Professional Print Buying

Phil Green
Editor

Graphic Arts Technical Foundation
PITTSBURGH

Graphic Arts Technical Foundation
200 Deer Run Road
Sewickley, PA 15143-2328
Phone: 412/741-6860
Fax: 412/741-2311
Email: info@gatf.lm.com
Internet: http://www.gatf.lm.com

Contents

Preface

Successful print buying draws on a wide mix of commercial and technical skills, and the individuals invited to contribute to this book bring a mature perspective on their own individual specialties. Each has experience in teaching as well as a depth of experience and a contemporary practice of great relevance to the issues discussed.

The focus throughout is on getting better value from the print purchasing transaction, from the initial stages of negotiating price and contract, through the briefing of suppliers and the management of design and prepress, the selection of materials, proofing, and quality control of the final product.

As a result, this book does not cover the basics of the printing processes nor preparing work for print (a range of titles that cover this ground can be found in the bibliography), but rather addresses the issues that people who buy print need to understand: how to negotiate better contracts with suppliers, for example, or how to make the most of the changing technology in printing and prepress.

All the contributors are willing to discuss the issues raised in this book, and their contact details can be found at the back. Alternatively, comments and suggestions for the next edition can be sent directly to me.

I would like to express my gratitude to all those who have assisted in the genesis of this book.

Phil Green

1 Introduction

Phil Green

For many organizations print is one of the largest external purchases (and for some organizations, such as publishers, it is indeed the main purchase). Because it has such a large influence on how the organization communicates with potential customers, it is arguably the most critical. Few other activities play such a powerful role in the public perception of an organization and its products. Print is therefore of substantial value to the organization. For any given communication need, the possible solutions are almost unlimited, and maximizing the value of the communication, at the lowest possible cost, is the central task of the print buyer.

Putting ink on paper is, of course, only one dimension of this communication activity, often the final stage in a long process. For this reason, print buying cannot truly be said to be a profession in itself. There are no officially recognized qualifications in print buying as there are in purchasing, for example. Most people who buy print (and the number of people who buy print at some time or another is in fact very large) do so in order to realize other goals — goals that may include promoting, marketing, publishing, informing and educating. Unless the organization has chosen to subdivide roles, the person who buys print is often primarily a communicator rather than a specialist in purchasing or production.

Because print buying is a unique type of purchasing activity, it demands an unusual mix of skills. The mix will vary according to the organization and its products, but the principal skills will usually include the following:

- The ability to negotiate with both external suppliers and internal colleagues
- Project management skills, including the ability to manage budgets and schedules
- An understanding of production processes

A wide knowledge base is needed to support these skills, ranging from commercial practice and legal requirements to a familiarity with the goals of the organization and an understanding of the technology of reproduction.

The range of skills required continues to change and evolve, as ways of doing business alter and developments in technology redefine the products and the methods of producing them. However, the emphasis needs to be on using these skills to extract value from the purchasing chain rather than just on understanding topics such as commerce, law, design or technology. It is this need to integrate skills from a wide range of disciplines that makes print buying a challenging and stimulating role. Print buying is undergoing significant changes, documented more extensively in the chapters that follow. Many of these changes are underpinned by the digital revolution in communication and reproduction technology; examples include the following:

- The print buyer now has a much wider range of suppliers to choose from as developments in communications technology open up the possibility of dealing with suppliers worldwide and make selection less constrained by geography.
- Organizations have moved many aspects of production in-house as the tools available on desktop computers make it possible to carry out many of the functions that were formerly the province of the skilled prepress worker.
- New ways of communicating are made possible by these changes in technology. For example, it is possible to add variable data to a printed piece, making it possible to customize it according to what is known about the intended recipient. The increasing cost-effectiveness of short runs (even of quality color printing) makes it possible to conceive of new products, or new ways of producing and distributing existing products.
- The production and distribution model is radically altered. It is no longer necessary to print centrally in quantity for distribution and for stock, since the speed and cost of data transfer make it more economical to distribute a product in digital form and have it reproduced locally. Moreover, production and communication technology support the reduction of stock levels to a minimum through just-in-time ordering.

In light of these changes the print buyer is faced with a number of strategic decisions which must be continually reviewed in order to ensure the value of printed products to the organization is maximized.

Make or buy. An organization that purchases print can bring an increasing number of activities in-house, including design and prepress. The attractions of vertical integration include increased control and the possibility of reduced costs, but against this must be weighed the inevitable cost of supporting such specialist activities, in staff and equipment as well as the need to devote resources to managing them. For some organizations the opportunity to create value internally and reduce external costs is a deciding factor, while in others the business culture may demand outsourcing whenever possible.

Media choice. For most communications, some form of printed product is the first choice. However, the increasing penetration of personal computers makes other media choices possible, including CD-ROM and online publishing through the Internet.

Supplier relations. Partnerships with suppliers are increasingly considered to be of critical importance in maximizing value. Buying print is often an intensely personal activity, and building the right relationships with suppliers can be a painstaking process.

Exploiting technology. Printing technology is advancing rapidly, and each new development brings with it opportunities for reducing the cost or enhancing the value of printed products. The print buyer does not need to become an expert in printing technology, but does need to keep abreast of the opportunities created by the latest advances.

Workflow

The production of a printed piece requires a series of separate stages in production, all of which demand specialized equipment and expertise to complete. An example is shown in Figure 1-1.

First there will be the briefing of the designer and the realization of the initial concept, followed by the preparation of the different elements of the design, including the writing of the copy, the selection of pictures (whether commissioned or sourced through external picture libraries or internal image databases) and the preparation of illustrations and

Figure 1-1.
Typical production
workflow.

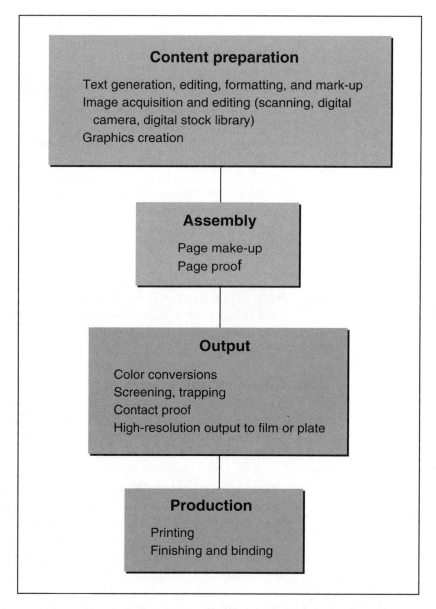

other graphics. Next will be the assembly of these different
elements into completed pages, and their output to film.
Page films are then imposed in register onto clear plastic
sheets for platemaking. Plates are mounted onto the press,
made ready, and the required number of copies are printed.
Finally, printed sections are folded, secured by stitching or
gluing, and trimmed to produce finished copies ready for
packing and dispatch.

Although this is a typical workflow, it is by no means universal. Reprints, for example, usually involve just minor changes to the text plates, while for different processes the stages in production may be quite different.

The complex production cycle means that the time from initial concept to delivery of the finished product is quite lengthy, and detailed attention to project management is required. Costs must be controlled and a series of approval points established to ensure that the integrity of the design is maintained through to the finished product.

It may be beneficial to consider strategies for simplifying the production cycle in order to make it easier to manage. The print buyer should weigh the advantages of using a single supplier against the possible cost benefits of contracting with suppliers separately. There may also be the possibility of bringing part (or even all) of the workflow in-house by taking advantage of the increasing availability of prepress equipment and software that runs on desktop computers and the introduction of high-volume printing systems such as Xerox's DocuTech.

Advanced digital production systems make it possible to omit some production stages:

- It is becoming more common for pages to be imposed electronically and output as a single piece of film ready for platemaking.
- Computer-to-plate systems enable the printer to impose pages electronically and image them directly onto the plates without having to make films, and direct-to-press systems go a step further by avoiding the need for plates.
- Printing digitally eliminates all intermediate stages between page make-up and printing.

Price and cost. Most pricing systems are based on charging the customer for the time spent directly on the different stages in the production workflow, together with the costs of the materials used and any subcontracted work. These are implemented through hourly cost rates for each type of work, with expensive equipment and highly skilled labor tending to have the highest rates. The printer is therefore in the business of selling time although, from the print buyer's point of view, it is not time but products that are being purchased. This mismatch between the unit of sale and the unit of purchase underlies some of the ambiguities in communicating a price estimate.

It is important to appreciate that the price for an activity, while linked to the printer's costs, is also based on an awareness of the price that exists in the market.

In analyzing the production workflow and the printer's costing structure, it is possible to distinguish between the fixed and variable elements in production. Up to the point when the plates are mounted on the press, the production time is the same regardless of the number of copies. From this point on, production time depends entirely on the number of copies produced. Other variable cost elements, like paper and ink, are also proportional to the quantity produced.

In other words, the fixed cost is the cost of the first copy, while the variable cost is the cost of each copy after that.

Therefore, the fixed cost element of the job does not change with the quantity, while the variable cost element is almost directly proportional to the quantity produced. There is much less room to reduce the variable costs of a job, since press speeds and paper costs can only be altered marginally. Fixed costs are much more elastic. The implication is that price competition between printers is focused more on the fixed cost element of the job.

The approval cycle. An approval cycle is a series of points through the production workflow at which different stages can be approved and signed off. Its purpose is to ensure that the finished product meets with the client's requirements and is satisfactory in every way. The approval cycle plays a key role in achieving value for money from the production processes, and allows you to minimize the possibility of error and reduce the cost of alterations.

The number of approval points will depend on the value of the job (either through its size or its relative importance to the organization), but will usually include a sign-off for each of the stages identified in the workflow diagram (Figure 1-1). A higher value job may require that the production stages shown be split into separate tasks in order to maintain tight control. More rigorous evaluation will also take place for high value work, with more iterations anticipated before approval is given.

The actual target of approval may be a document (such as a brief, a costing or a specification) or it may be a tangible proof of the end product of one stage in design or production (such as a design visual or a contact proof).

The approval cycle should be planned at the beginning of the job, as soon as the design has taken shape sufficiently to allow you to identify the critical stages. Everyone who will need to be involved in approval should be identified and their role agreed, as one of the most common problems that arise in producing a piece of visual communication is that people in an organization who have not been involved in its production want to make changes at a late stage. If this is a persistent problem the print buyer may need to get agreement, at an appropriate level of seniority, on how the approval cycle is to be managed.

The approval cycle should document who will give approval at each stage, the time scale for approval, and enough detail about what is being approved at each stage. Checklists can be employed to make the approval process more consistent and reliable.

Innovation in Print Production and Print Buying

Value and excellence in visual communication are often achieved through innovation, and the print purchaser should, where possible, exploit innovative techniques of design or production to make a printed communication more successful.

Print production is undergoing a period of great change, as are communications and business systems generally. As a result there are many opportunities for innovation, and at the same time a need to continually adapt to and master new ways of doing things.

Developments in digital technology have created the possibility of new ways of creating and delivering the message. Print is still one of the media available (and for many products it is likely to continue to remain the dominant choice) but many organizations will find that alternative media such as CD-ROM or online publishing through the Internet will be more successful for some of their communications. In some cases mixed-media products are the best solution combining, for example, a CD with a printed brochure and packaging.

Some sectors of print are contracting (business forms, for example) as new ways of doing business supersede older methods but, overall, printing is an industry that continues to grow strongly and invest in the future. As a result of new technology the cost of print in real terms has been falling for many years, especially in the areas of color and short-run production.

Figure 1-2.
Different models of print and disribution are made possible by emerging technologies.

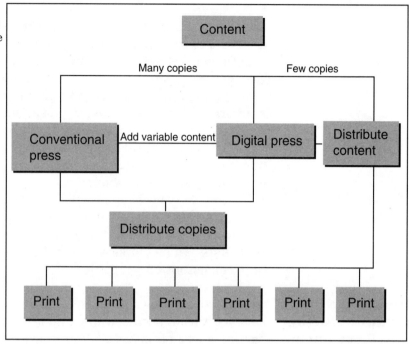

Innovations in the production process are capable of delivering significant advantages in quality, cost and speed of production. The consequence is a potential for radical improvement in existing products and the possibility of new products that exploit features of the new technologies.

New ways of working offer improvements in artwork preparation, design, illustration, photography, image capture and content management (through text-based and graphical databases and the use of document structuring technologies like standard generalized mark-up language or SGML). They also create benefits in print production and distribution.

Underlying many of the new technologies in print production is the digital revolution in prepress and printing (see Figure 1-2). To realize the maximum benefit an all-digital workflow up to the point of ink on paper is ideal, although in reality most printed pieces will continue to include non-digital stages, such as film, for some time to come.

Digital prepress and print make it possible to distribute the content of a communication electronically. Page files can be transmitted to a printer anywhere in the world, opening up new potential suppliers but also making it feasible to distribute a communication in digital form for local reproduction. Short-run digital print technologies also enable the purchaser to print "on demand," or even transfer the responsibility of printing to the end-user according to immediate need.

Innovations in print purchasing are by no means limited to the technological variety. New ways of doing business with suppliers are tending to emphasize the importance of building partnerships instead of the more traditional adversary model of trade. Innovative forms of contract, stock and purchasing strategies have also come to the fore, some underpinned by technological developments. For example, just-in-time purchasing is supported by electronic document interchange (EDI) that enables purchaser and supplier to exchange paperwork and payment electronically.

One of the newest innovations (and perhaps the one which in the future will be seen as the most significant in the changes it brings about in the activities of the print purchaser) is the move to doing business online. The advent of widespread communications links and standard communication protocols enables a variety of different forms of online trade, from the initial location of potential suppliers and exchanging specifications and estimates, through to transfer of job files for output and even the distribution of the final product as an online communication.

The whole of the print production process is one that lends itself to online transaction since every element of a printed product that goes into that product exists at some point as a digital file. The content of a communication, comprising text, illustrations and photographs, can readily be acquired and approved online. Writers and copy editors can exchange copy and revisions by email, graphic artists can send EPS files in the same way, and even photographs (which involve much

Table 1-1.
Some of the principal concerns of the print purchaser.

Briefing	Content	Approval
• Supplier selection • Creative brief • Changes • Production specification • Production schedule • Progress tracking	• Text generation and formatting • Graphics creation • Image acquisition through commissioning or stock • Editing • Alterations • Media • Structure	• Visualization of concept • Internal approval of content • Iterations to find optimum design solution • Corrections and alterations • Simulation of finished product

larger file sizes) can be sourced through digital picture libraries that allow the purchaser to browse and download low-resolution images and have the high-resolution versions sent directly to the printer.

The commercial aspects of print production are also capable of being handled online through intelligent Web search agents that can seek out estimates, and through electronic exchange of specifications, schedules and payments. Similarly, project management can be made more efficient by online interaction with the printer's management information system, for example, to find out the progress of current jobs and make changes in copy or specifications.

In all of the new ways of creating, producing and distributing visual communications that are described above, information plays a key role. The client–supplier partnership is increasingly bound up in the exchange of high-quality information whose purpose is to add the maximum value to the finished product.

All of the themes introduced in this chapter are expanded on in the chapters that follow.

2   Commercial and Legal Issues

Chris Conolly-Smith

Every print buyer must be aware of the commercial and legal implications of the print purchasing and control process. The print buyer enters into contracts:
- Approves the different stages of a project, often making changes during the course of production;
- Authorizes payment on completion and approval of the samples and the stock; and
- Follows the job during its ultimate usage to ensure that no problems ensue.

Contracts will involve the creation of films, disks, images and design, the ownership of all of which must be clearly stated and agreed. Above all, the contract reflects the agreement of the two parties, the supplier and the print buyer. The impact on third parties who are not signatories must also be taken into account.

From this it should not be inferred that every buyer must have an accounting or legal qualification. An accounting qualification does not make a buyer more commercial just as a legal qualification may not result in better or fairer contracts. The buyer needs a clear understanding of the issues and procedures involved, and a knowledge of when to seek expert advice.

Commercial Issues

The Costing System

Every printed product is unique and is priced accordingly. The actual price quoted will depend on a complex mix of factors including the time needed to carry out the work, the cost of the materials used, and the prices for similar work available from competitors. These can be summarized as cost factors and market factors.

Some printers still use a simple costing system to calculate prices, based on the cost of production plus a profit margin.

However, most now consider pricing strategy to be a management activity based as much on marketing as on costings, and in recent years many printers have adopted more aggressive, market-oriented alternatives. Nevertheless, an understanding of costs is still needed to arrive at a price, otherwise there is the danger that work will be taken on at a loss, or that orders will be lost through higher prices than are essential to the business.

The principal aim of any costing system is to ensure that all the costs of the business are recovered, through revenue from the work undertaken. A business uses its understanding of its costs to assist in making all kinds of strategic decisions, including investment and expansion, as well as providing a basis for the pricing system.

Successful printers base prices not on a simple estimate of cost, but on the contribution that the revenue will make to their business, including administration and production overhead and the cost of capital employed in the business.

The main types of costing systems operated by printers are known as absorption and marginal costing. Marginal costing systems encourage the printer to focus on the value of an order to the business, and tend to result in lower prices.

For the majority of printers, costs and prices are calculated by management information systems that hold continually updated information on the productivity of the different activities within the business, and are able to generate prices with detailed options very quickly. Some systems allow printers to choose between different costing methods, according to their perception of how price-sensitive the work is.

In reality there is a great deal of elasticity in a printer's costs, since every order that is accepted increases the utilization of the equipment and spreads the fixed costs of the business over a greater revenue, up to the point where the printer has to subcontract work in order to complete it.

On this analysis, where overtime working is required due to the pressure of work, it is actually cheaper for the printer since it reflects a higher capacity utilization of the fixed assets, which is of far greater importance than the wages premium involved. The surcharge that is often made to the customer is thus in reality a consequence of a marketing decision, rather than a reflection of the costs incurred. An example of price elasticity is shown in Table 2-1.

During periods of high demand the printer can choose to submit an estimate of $8,250 (£5,000) or more. In periods of

Table 2-1.
Example of price
structure for a printed
product.

Competitive price	$8,250	(£5,000)
Direct costs (materials, manufacturing labor, subcontracted work)	$4,950	(£3,000)
Indirect costs (administration, marketing, etc.)	$2,393	(£1,450)
Profit	**$907**	**(£550)**

low capacity utilization, a dramatic price reduction of up to $2,393 (£1,450) would still show a benefit to the company, as it would contribute to paying for the manufacturing labor costs. The printer must, of course, take care not to erode the customer's perception of price levels too far.

Note that price elasticity is less applicable to those direct costs whose price is determined externally, such as materials and subcontract work.

Many printers who are now well established in the international print scene have forced their way into the market by aggressive pricing, using costing systems of the kind described above.

Pricing

Through skilled marketing a printer will seek to price jobs using market pricing. Estimates will be priced according to the value provided to supply customers' needs. Market research and a close understanding of the customers' organizations, and the business environment in which they compete, are essential.

Return-on-capital pricing. While the above methods of costing and pricing operate on the bases of costs and percentages of sales revenue, return-on-capital pricing starts from the fact that a printer seeks to make an annual return on invested capital. The methods described earlier do not take into account the levels of capital employed but assume that the printer wishes to achieve a minimum net profit on sales revenue. For example, one printer may aim for a net profit on sales of 11%, while another has a target of a return on investment of 20% on capital.

Applied to printers' prices, this technique would encourage printers to value fast turnaround jobs which can be completed, invoiced and paid for quickly. Any working capital (films, plates, paper) is then tied up for shorter periods. As with other techniques, the success of this pricing system depends heavily on the capacity utilization of the factory (see Figure 2-1).

Print jobs for customers who pay promptly and supply their own paper are potentially more profitable and can be priced more aggressively. Some printers prefer to supply paper because they can ensure its suitability for their equipment, and because they can add a profit margin to the paper cost.

Cash flow pricing. Not a technique in itself, cash flow pricing looks at the amount of cash, rather than profit, generated by the acceptance of a job. Printers may value cash flow over trading profits in the short term, both in periods of expansion where cash is needed to finance increases in working capital, and in recessionary periods where revenues are reduced. Depreciation on printing equipment does not affect cash flows; the use of standard papers and plates will, in the short term, reduce stock levels and hence generate cash, while skilled labor costs have to be paid for even if the factory is not full.

Other factors in pricing. Many printers have workloads that fluctuate dramatically. Overheads that are not fully recovered from sales still have to be paid for. This problem may be dealt with by a seasonal pricing policy that offers discounts on prices quoted at other times in the year. Conversely, at peak times printers may well seek to improve margins through higher prices.

The printer's problem is similar to that of a railroad or airline. Customers to whom the train or airline is essential need the transportation provided. Other passengers, for example at off-peak times, need to be persuaded to travel by train or air with a particular airline. The train or aircraft will carry out its journey regardless of whether it has empty seats. The printer has the same problem regarding price perceptions. It does not want to encourage its existing valued customers to demand price reductions when they hear that their printer is offering lower prices to other customers with a smaller volume of work of an intermittent nature.

Many of the most significant technical developments in the printing industry have focused on reducing start-up costs: platemaking, makeready costs, and paper waste before the first copies are produced. These technical innovations bring three benefits:

Figure 2-1.
Top Printers costs are made up of the above elements (proportions vary according to the type of work).

Bottom The costs of a printed piece are made up of a combination of fixed cost (shaded) and variable cost (unshaded) elements.

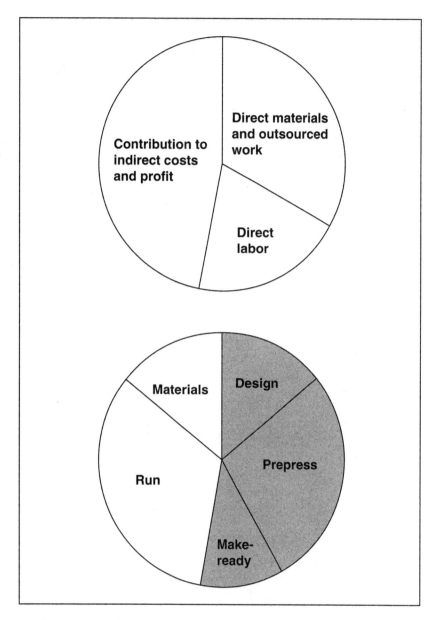

- They make the printer more competitive on short print runs
- They increase the printer's productive capacity leading to higher revenues per year
- They reduce hourly cost rates as overheads are apportioned over a greater output level.

Costing and Pricing Systems: A Summary

All of these methods can be combined to produce an estimate. A printer must be able to analyze costs in detail and also be aware of market prices. Estimation should not be seen as a mathematical or purely technical function but rather part of the commercial and marketing function.

The impact of the points discussed above is that the gap has widened between the price that a printer wants to charge and the price that the market will permit. This is because the percentage of fixed costs in a quotation, including depreciation of expensive electronically controlled machinery, has increased significantly. While increased labor efficiency and use of new technology have improved the competitive position of many North American and British printers, the need for strong marketing has increased. It is perhaps the realization of this need, combined with an improved response to the needs of the client, that has allowed many printers to strengthen their position with respect to international competition.

A Price Database

Printing is not a commodity that can be traded, and estimates for print and paper are not quoted publicly. Buyers compare prices among trusted colleagues in other firms, but may sometimes doctor their statements if they are reluctant to appear to be paying more than similar firms. There is, in practice, no automatic connection between the size of the buying organization and the price paid. The motivation of the buyer and its rapport with and loyalty to key printers are often more influential in setting price levels.

Many buyers will have computer estimating systems based either on printers' price scales or on past estimates. However, these will not give the current market prices, and it is vital that a buyer be able to develop, access and interrogate a database of prices for different job types, and that the printer be aware of this database. Printers will almost certainly respond by more consistent pricing. (Consistent pricing, however, does not mean that estimates always vary in the same way according to the print run, but rather according to the market, i.e., to customer needs and perceptions.)

Printers normally maintain their own database of prices submitted, with details of which ones were accepted and which rejected, within their management information system. They will also track their competitors' prices.

Evaluating Estimates

Any full comparison of two or more printing estimates must include an analysis of differences in the financial and commercial terms. These involve subjective judgments of risk and service, which are concepts that some buying organizations find difficult to accept. They feel duty bound to accept the lowest bid. The aim of the additional analysis recommended below is to ensure that the best estimate is also the lowest invoice for the required job and quality within the agreed schedule.

A buyer looks for a consistent level of price estimates and invoices in order to establish confidence between buyer and printer. In the longer term it must, however, be profitable for both the printer and customer.

The aim of any analysis must be to assess the best supplier for the job. In certain cases, the lowest price will be the objective, in others the fastest delivery, and in others the best quality. The parameters will change according to the objectives of the organization and with each individual job.

Many organizations still insist that buyers accept the lowest estimate. Others will allow the buyer to make a qualitative judgment in order to assess the best, or most appropriate, supplier. A typical objective comparison of two estimates is shown in Table 2-2.

Table 2-2.
Comparison between two estimates.

	Supplier A	Supplier B
Credit terms	30	60
Payment method	check	letter of credit
Country	U.S.	Europe
Terms	delivered domicile	area delivered
Currency	U.S. dollar	local
Risk-Firm Price?	Firm	Firm
Lead-time (days)	14	30
Basic price ($)	82,500	75,900
Credit terms ($)	0	(759)
Invoice extras forecast ($)	825	0
Couriers ($)	0	495
Freight on samples ($)	0	247.50
Extra transport ($)	0	825
Stock risk ($)	0	1,650
Control risk ($)	0	825
Quality risk ($)	0	0
Currency risk ($)	0	2,277
Likely invoice value ($)	83,325	81,460.50
Savings ($)		1,864.50
Savings (%)		2.2

The aim of this analysis at estimate stage is to assess the likely job cost after receiving all invoices, in order to assess the best option for the organization. A growing number of organizations will allow buyers to evaluate quotations in this way. Buyers are frequently asked to carry out a research and development function, and to make qualitative buying decisions on print and media purchasing. Increasingly they are no longer a service function but a profit center.

Other Commercial Negotiating Strategies

Volume discounts. A volume discount based on the turnover produced with a particular printer acts as an incentive for both parties without contractual commitment. Printing companies dislike buyers who promise a large volume of work each year that does not materialize, and as a result some offer volume discounts only on the basis of actual turnover.

Phased deliveries. Many buying organizations do not need the total print run to be delivered immediately on completion, but over several weeks or months. A deal may stipulate that deliveries and invoices are to be phased according to a set delivery schedule. The contract should stipulate whether the buyer has the right to make copy changes on later deliveries, or whether the printer can print in a single run.

Capacity booking. Magazine and newspaper publishers require guaranteed delivery schedules. They obtain very competitive prices because of this commitment, and, because of the cash cycle of magazine and newspaper sales, do not need the longer credit required by some buying organizations. The pagination of each issue, however, will vary from issue to issue depending on advertising revenue.

Price scales. Under this method, prices are agreed for a fixed period, usually one year. Thus both organizations can focus on production and marketing issues, and on minimizing down stock levels. There will usually be a letter of intent concerning anticipated turnover levels. This avoids negotiation over each individual job, and is ideal for standardized regular work. If market prices rise, the buyer benefits; if market prices fall, the printer is able to maintain price levels although the buyer may reduce the volume of work placed with that printer.

Other Financial Considerations for the Buyer

The buyer must analyze the total cost of the job. This may include the following:
- The time taken to brief suppliers, request estimates, negotiate and gain internal approval to proceed
- The time taken to record, authorize, and pay printers' invoices within the organization
- Storage costs and the cost (and risk) of holding stock
- The risk of going out of stock
- The value of the job to the organization, and the loss that could occur if the brief is not met adequately or in time
- The capacity utilization of internal creative and print resources
- The impact on morale within the organization, especially within the marketing and sales departments, of delivering late or of delivering poor quality items.

Payment Methods and Terms

Credit terms. The aim of credit terms is to encourage the buyer to purchase more, and to partially or completely fund stock levels. It also allows the buyer time to check the bulk stock in the buyer's warehouse before payment is made. It is essential that the buyer understand the effective credit period. Table 2-3 illustrates this point.

Readers can apply their own local trading terms to evaluate relevant comparisons. Where the end-user is some distance from the buying organization, then the effective credit may sometimes be increased by the use of a printer closer to the user.

In general, printers will invoice on completion and allow credit. Where a new customer is being served for the first time, or where a job has a long lead-time or is delayed, the printer may hope to request stage payments. Now that many

Table 2-3.
Examples of different credit periods (days).

Agreement terms	Credit terms	Shipping time to warehouse	Facility to defer payment	Effective credit
Local printer, payment by check				
	30	1	~7	36
Local printer, payment by letter of credit				
	30	1	0	29
Foreign printer, payment by check				
	60	25	7	42
Foreign printer, payment by letter of credit				
	60	25	0	35

print buyers submit film or disks (rather than hard-copy text or illustrations as in the past), and printers are in a more competitive business, lead times have become much shorter. Thus the justification for advance or stage payment is reduced. If they cannot be avoided, the contract and documentation should (where possible) be checked by a legal adviser. In addition, the printer should be asked to supply evidence of its financial standing.

Overdue interest. Many countries now allow, by law, for the supplier to demand interest at an agreed rate on overdue payments. Where such regulations do not override other contractual agreements, a supplier cannot demand interest on late payment unless this is provided for in the contract and its appendices. The buyer may need to scan carefully the terms and conditions of estimate from each printer. A growing number of buyers now issue contracts with their own (reasonable) terms and conditions of order. These will state in many cases that they override the terms of the printer's estimate.

Prompt payment discounts. Suppliers may offer discounts in order to persuade the buyer to pay earlier. Certain organizations have been known to take the discount and still pay late, and negotiations should include this point. Early payment discounts do, of course, force the buyer to approve invoices quickly in order to take advantage of the discount. Payment by letter of credit or bill of exchange (discussed later in this chapter) rules out such clauses, unless agreed prior to the letter being drawn up and included in the contract.

Electronic funds transfer. Larger organizations are now reengineering their whole purchasing and accounting systems in order to streamline operations. Increasingly such organizations are paying by electronic funds transfer whereby payments, once approved by the buying organization, are credited to the supplier's account electronically. This reduces paperwork and speeds up payments. This applies in particular to repeat work, which can be authorized on the computer if certain agreed terms (such as quantity and price) are as stated in the contract. The potential administrative savings of systems such as EDI (electronic document interchange) are such that some organizations will only deal with suppliers that use them.

International Issues

Both demand for and supply of printing are on an international scale. Buyers contract with non-local printers in order to gain a competitive advantage on price, service, unique facilities, or local delivery to customers located near the printer. Thus a European customer may send films to a North American printer and the output will be distributed throughout the North American market. It is often easier, quicker and cheaper to transport film or digital data than finished products. Many fast emerging young economies are investing heavily in new printing factories and sometimes have indigenous sources of pulp. For printers these young economies have the potential to represent:

- New sources of supplies; and
- New sources of custom.

One might conclude that buyers would source all printing in areas of cheap labor with undervalued currencies. However, developed economies are able to attract priority supply of paper at attractive prices, and are able to afford the latest high-output printing equipment and thus narrow the labor cost differentials. This means that countries in Europe and North America can often compete equally on contracts, and are able to guarantee supply in times of rising materials prices.

The administration of print jobs in more remote print locations will usually add to administration and control costs, and sometimes to risk. Clear planning and communication are essential. During the early phases of a printer-buyer relationship, whether with local or foreign printers, the printer will not understand all the needs of the buyer. The buyer must resolve this by comprehensive briefings and documentation. These factors should be built in to any estimate comparisons before the final selection of printer is made.

The risk must be quantified and in some cases may be the overriding factor. Late delivery of products for seasonal or time-sensitive markets may mean a significant loss of profits for the buying company and loss of market share. Longer lead-times from more remote printers may mean that the buying company must hold higher stocks. This creates a risk that the higher stock levels will result in stock write-offs if demand patterns change. Such write-offs can be much greater than the print savings. Where the buying unit is judged on profits rather than on costs saved, the policy is made easier.

Each country has its own legal system, and both buyers and printers will inevitably wish to insist that contracts are drawn up under the laws and jurisdiction (including arbitration) of their own country. The larger the buyer, the more likely it is that the contract will be drawn up under the laws of the buyer's country. This must be agreed rather than simply added to the terms of the order, which is then disputed throughout the printing cycle.

Any new supplier represents a risk, and perhaps a greater risk if remote from the buyer's country. This risk can be reduced, in part, by following a series of stages towards a successful conclusion.

Approval stages. The printer should be instructed to:
- Confirm receipt of film, that any films and proofs received are acceptable (including sample proofing for a repeat job, since ink standards cannot be assumed to be universal, nor the sequence of printing colors)
- Supply bluelines of text and illustration film
- Supply samples for written approval (sheets, finished products, packing materials).

Legal aspects. Both parties will seek to negotiate a contract drawn up under the law of their country. In most cases the contract will be drawn up under the law of the buyer, using the standard terms and conditions of the buyer's organization, after lengthy discussion and explanation. Arbitration procedures must be laid down under the standard conditions.

Financial information. Details of the printer's financial and trading position should be sought, including:
- Share capital
- Directors and shareholders
- The printer's bankers
- Credit checks and ratings
- Personal recommendations.

Communication. An insistence on the use of English (or the buyer's native language) for all correspondence and meetings is essential, and the supplier should have customer service representatives available who can communicate fluently with the buyer, and who understand the customer's needs. The availability of modern communication technologies is also essential; these may include ISDN lines, email and Internet links, as well as the traditional courier services to a local sales office and directly to the buyer's offices.

Where a local representative is involved, the buyer must be clear whether this is an agency or a sales office, and must contract with the relevant party as advised by its department.

Foreign Currency Risk

The buyer has the following main choices in managing the currency risk involved in purchasing overseas:
- To purchase in the buyer's currency
- To purchase in the supplier's local currency
- To purchase in an agreed third currency
- To acquire an option to purchase the amount of local currency needed for maturity on the due date for payment
- To buy forward the amount of local currency needed.

Purchasing in the buyer's currency. This places the currency risk with the printer, who may as a result increase prices. The printer would seek to penalize delays which could lead to currency losses. Where the buyer is in a rich country, the printer may prefer to quote in the buyer's currency.

Local currency purchasing. The printer will add no margin for risk when quoting in the local currency, and may therefore produce more competitive quotations. Depending on currency movements between the price being agreed and payment being made, the buyer may then either end up paying more than the original budget, or alternatively may make an additional profit if the buying organization has access to good currency market insight.

Use of a third currency. The use of the U.S. dollar is common in international contracts not involving U.S. printers. The buying organization may have receipts in U.S. dollars from subsidiaries or customers and may seek to match receipts and payments.

Options. The buying organizations will take out an option to buy an agreed amount of a currency on a particular date and a fixed price. No money is paid out. The risk is then with the bank or other institution offering the option. Delays will necessitate the rolling on of this option under new contracts.

Buying forward. The purchasing organization will "buy forward" the amount of the local currency required. Forward buying entails the transfer of funds into another currency, and interest can still be earned. If the delivery is early or delayed, no roll-on contracts are necessary.

Many buying organizations will place the responsibility for the management of currency risk with the treasury department, which will lay down the policy to be adopted. Subject to the trading and international nature of the organization, the policy may be different in different continents. The organization may insist that the buying department adopt a policy of accepting no risk. Whatever the policy, the buyer will normally have to communicate all orders to the treasury function, since few organizations will allow the purchasing department to formulate the currency exposure policy.

Payment Methods

Printers' estimates need to be read carefully, and negotiation and agreements must include the credit terms and method of payment.

Letters of credit. By comparison with bills of exchange, letters of credit are signed at contract rather than at invoice stage. The buyer agrees to pay a fixed amount of money at a set future date, subject to the agreed terms being adhered to. These terms might include job specifications, color quality or paper samples. Tolerances would be stated concerning unders and overs, maximum number of days delay permitted, materials weight and other items of clearly definable importance to the buyer.

A typical letter of credit is the irrevocable letter of credit (IRLC). This reduces the risk of non-payment considerably as the buyer's bank will usually subtract the amount from the buyer's overdraft limit from the date of signature.

In all the above cases, the buyer will want to confer with both the finance or treasury function and with legal advisers. Subject to their advice, the buyer may wish to include the payments terms and methods on the request-for-estimates sent out when seeking quotations.

Bill of exchange. The printer submits a document under which the customer agrees to pay a fixed amount (the invoice or part of the invoice) at a fixed future date. The customer accepts the bill and sends it back to the supplier, often via the bank. The supplier can then either hold the bill until the due date, or sell the bill to a third party. Often shipping documents will be released only on acceptance of the bill (this is known as a closed bill). Where trust has been established, open bills will be used and the shipping documents will be sent in advance of, and separate from, the bill of exchange.

Bills of exchange are widely used in Europe and Asia, and indeed in most of the world outside North America, where letters of credit are preferred. It is quite acceptable for bills to be used with local suppliers. The contract must state that this is to be the means of payment as the method cannot be changed unilaterally at a later date. Bills of exchange, which are signed at the invoice stage, do not guarantee payment as they can be reneged on, but they do ensure prompt payment once signed. The buyer's bank account is debited only on the due date.

Legal Issues

This chapter does not seek to explain the laws that affect print buyers but rather to highlight some of the issues that the print buyer commonly faces, which should be discussed either with a legal adviser within the organization or with an outside specialist lawyer. Most issues can be resolved by clear planning, good communication and a clear understanding of what is being asked, and of what each supplier is providing in the form of a service or finished product. In particular it is essential to assess the ultimate aims and usage of each job or product — how and where it will be used.

The vast majority of disputes can be resolved between the parties without external lawyers. Occasionally specialist experts or arbitrators are called upon to recommend a solution, and even serious disputes can usually be resolved by a brief consultation with legal experts, or by a single exchange of lawyers' letters.

Contracts with Suppliers

The implementation of formal standard contracts for all transactions (or a series of standard contracts for specific purposes), drawn up by internal experts or a specialist legal firm, is a prerequisite to sound contracts. These documents should be prepared in consultation with major suppliers and should take into account customs of the trade. The process of drawing up standard contracts forces the buyer to study all the stages, terms, issues and implications. The process of drawing up such contracts will be beneficial only if the firm enters into all its contracts with sound firms on fair and commercial lines. Here commercial aspects, comprising financial and risk factors, blend with legal aspects.

A Contract Checklist

It is a good practice to draw up a checklist of items to consider and include in all negotiations and contracts. In many organizations, nonstandard contracts must be referred to an internal legal department.

Any checklist should include an in-depth study of the suitability of the supplier, and the exact nature of the deal.

Supplier audit. Apart from technical aspects, an audit should include:
- The supplier's experience in carrying out similar work for your market
- Its financial status, directors and shareholders, charges against assets (including the status of the supplier's contact within the organization, and of the proposed signatory of the contract)
- A check to ensure that the organization submitting the quotation is the same firm as the contracting organization, and to whom payment will be made.

You should take expert advice on the role of agents and local offices, and should ask your supplier's head office about the status of such agents or local offices.

The deal. In most print jobs, it might appear that it is easy to describe the deal. However, most disputes arise from lack of attention to detail in this area. Examples include:
- Individual responsibilities: who will supply paper, samples and proofs; who pays for freight and customs clearance; whether subcontracting is permitted
- Technical aspects (for example, the type of films or disks to be submitted)
- Supply of materials: what must be supplied by the print buyer in order to allow the supplier to complete the contract, and what the supplier must provide to other organizations in the production chain
- Disputes: how problems that emerge after delivery and acceptance, or after payment has been made, will be resolved
- Insurance and third-party issues.

The price. The unit and total price inclusive of local and other taxes should be checked. Is the price firm? What does the price include? Is delivery included?

Terms and conditions. Most large buying organizations will impose their own standard conditions upon suppliers regardless of the industry from which they are purchasing. Many of the points identified in this checklist will be covered in such terms and conditions, which will usually state that the buyer's standard conditions override those of the printer (which will appear on the estimate). Many industry and supplier representative groups recommend their own standard conditions to their members, but these should not be considered non-negotiable. The law of supply and demand applies here, but the conditions must be fair. Most buyers will agree their standard conditions with new suppliers before any work is placed.

Delivery. Delivery applies to the delivery of services, artwork, disks and images, as well as the finished product. The contract should state how delivery is to be satisfactorily carried out and accepted. To what destinations are deliveries to be made? What is acceptable proof of delivery — delivery notes signed by a customer or shipping documents? Must delivery be made in entirety before payment becomes due? What has to be proven in order to ensure that payment will be authorized? What redress does the buyer have against non-delivery or faulty delivery?

Schedule. The schedule should ideally be part of the contract. To be fair and enforceable, it must include dates for completion of agreed operations by both parties, which means that dates for the delivery of films or the approval of proofs by the buyer must also be included.

Any contract should lay down or explain acceptable tolerances on the schedule. In many cases, a few hours or days may not be vital; in other jobs time may be "of the essence." The negotiations and the subsequent contract should state this clearly in order to protect the buyer. All buyers should consult with their legal advisers on this aspect.

Tolerances. The two parties must define what are acceptable tolerances given the customs of the trade, the nature of the buyer's business, and the supplier's machinery and trade. Examples of these are:

- Overs and unders (is the supplier permitted to deliver and charge for 110 instead of 100 items)
- The use of alternative papers.

Tolerances on paper weight and caliper will usually be included in the standard conditions of the buyer organization. These tolerances must be reasonable given the industry in question and the technology available.

Title and ownership. Does title to the goods pass to the buyer organization on delivery? Can the supplier sell the goods to another party if the buyer refuses to pay? Who owns items created in the process of carrying out the contract, such as disks, programs, templates, drawings, images, films, and the arrangement of text and pictures? These items will normally be the property of their creator unless specified otherwise in the contract.

Payment. This has been discussed more fully in the earlier section. From the legal angle the following questions must also be raised:

- Are there any laws in the country under whose legislation the contract is drawn up which are enforceable (such as those concerning statutory interest on late payments)?;
- On what grounds can the buyer justifiably delay or refuse payment?
- How can a buyer demand the return of advance payments made against work that is not carried out satisfactorily?;
- How can a buyer protect the organization against faults that come to light after payment has been made to the supplier in full?

Warranties and penalties. The supplier will confirm its ability to enter into the contract and to perform it, and that likely problems will be resolved in an agreed way. These clauses protect the buyer against certain third-party risks.

Legislation. Regardless of the supplier's location, most buying organizations will seek to enter into contracts which are subject to their own countries' legislation and arbitration.

Many of the topics discussed above can be included in the standard terms and conditions of the buyer's organization.

They will need to be brought to the attention of new suppliers and agreed before any work is placed. Once agreed, these terms and conditions can then be applied to all contracts.

Litigation

Buying organizations must understand the recourse open to them and to their suppliers (and the buyer's customers) when a contract breaks down or is voided. In particular they must be aware of the costs and time spans involved. They must be prepared to sue, or appear to be prepared to sue, when they are the suffering party. Prevention and common-sense solutions are the preferred solutions, as any litigation is expensive and time-consuming. Most disputes can be solved between the two parties, while a few need an exchange of lawyers' letters. Only rarely is arbitration or court action necessary, and in many cases commercial pressure or the need for cash will encourage one of the parties to seek a settlement.

Arbitration clauses are essential as they produce faster, less expensive and less emotional solutions. The use of independent expert organizations (such as Pira International) can assist in resolving issues more quickly and out of court.

Quality

It is perhaps impossible to define what quality means in a legal sense. The emphasis should be on clearly briefing the supplier so that there can be no doubt about the work they are contracted to carry out. Specifications should include all the details that matter to the finished product.

For creative work, the contract should lay down clearly the purpose of the job, and the supply of roughs or other elements for approval. Roughs or briefing notes may be included as addenda to contracts.

Different countries will have legislation covering specific aspects of quality, particularly in the packaging field. Food and pharmaceuticals are both examples of industries where the need to protect the customer has resulted in rigorous legal requirements about the content and consistency of the printing.

In practice, schedule and quality issues form the main legal stumbling blocks for buyers. The finished job may be disappointing, and the buyer instructed to reject, even though the supplier has met the terms of the contract.

Many problems emerge after a job has been delivered. For example, a paper may discolor due to moisture or specification, or the strength of the finishing may prove inadequate

---

PRINTING ORDER

To Great Impressions, Inc.

Date xx.xx.xx

Job Number 56789
Buyer Code 08
Product Code 1009

These must be quoted on all correspondence, shipping documents, packing or cartons (including bar codes), and invoices

Please supply 20,000 copies for the agreed firm price of $33,000 delivered customer's warehouse cleared. This equates to a price of $1.65 per copy for the first 20,000 copies. Additional copies as permitted within the contract will be invoiced at $1.32 per copy.

Details are enclosed in the Appendices which form part of this contract. These appendices include:

1. The specification attached (Appendix A).
2. The agreed terms and conditions of the buyer (Appendix B), which override the terms of the printer's estimate. These include acceptable tolerances on items such as overs and unders, paper weight and caliper.
3. The agreed schedule (Appendix C).
4. Shipping and transport specification and requirements (Appendix D).
5. Packing requirements (Appendix E).

Specifically, but not exclusively, the price includes:

- checking films
- supplying a final proof for approval before printing
- supplying blank paper samples for approval
- printed samples for approval before shipment
- supplying paper, board, inks
- courier and air freight costs to and from the buyer
- transfer of ownership to the buyer of all films and disks involved in the printing and completion of the job

The schedule:

The date contained in the schedule (Appendix C) is very important to the buyer due to a promotion scheduled to begin on xx.xx.xx, 5 days after the agreed delivery date into the buyer's warehouse.

Payment and credit terms:

45 days from delivery and acceptance of each delivery according to the schedule. Delivery to follow written approval of samples. Payment by check (or letter of credit, electronic transfer, etc., as appropriate). If the buyer pays within 15 days of each invoice, a 2.5% discount may be taken.

Signed by a duly authorized signatory of the Customer (both copies).

Signed by a duly authorized signatory of the Printer (both copies)

Figure 2-2. A typical printing contract.

when delivered into the retail shops. The customer may have paid for the goods already, and in this situation the supplier tends to be motivated more by the prospect of future work than by legal considerations.

Content

This section outlines copyright, licenses and ownership issues, as well as libel and "passing off." Since readers of this book will be in different continents with different legal systems, and will operate within specialist industries with varying customs of trade, this section does not seek to be a legal guide, nor should it be seen as definitive. It aims merely to highlight certain key issues, how and when to take advice, and how to manage the content issues. Print buyers must develop their own policies according to their needs and operations.

The following is a possible action plan for a print buyer who has just taken over responsibility within a new organization and whose job involves commissioning copy, pictures, sound and multimedia.

1. Establish the needs of typical jobs in terms of copy, pictures, design. Agree with management whether to buy or license material. Agree on the contractual period, the geographical area, the media for licensing or purchase, and reuse terms.

2. Obtain and read copies of typical contracts used in the same business sector, and any standard contracts and precedents that have been published; obtain standard contracts written by trade associations such as printers, authors, photographers and artists. Assimilate their contents and customize them to the needs of your organization in a reasonable fashion. Many trade organizations register their contracts in order to ensure that they do not contain unfair terms which would be ruled out in any legal solution to a dispute.

3. Instruct legal advisers within the organization or under instruction from the organization to devise standard contracts for authors, designers, artists, and photographers in a user-friendly style.

4. Draw up "friendly but firm" standard contracts for regular activities. Arrange training sessions with regular suppliers over the new contracts and procedures.

5. Draw up guideline documentation for staff and suppliers. Allow time for training relevant staff and informing key suppliers.

6. Implement internal controls to ensure that buyers work strictly to the standard contracts, and that all variations are agreed at the appropriate level and with internal or external legal advisers.

What is being purchased. A print buyer can buy outright for exclusive use, or acquire the right to use the material exclusively (or nonexclusively) for a specific use within a limited period or geographical area. The material, text, picture or design may be specifically commissioned for the buyer's organization, or may be in existence already. Material may also be originated by internal staff, working officially but in some cases outside normal hours for additional payment.

Duties of suppliers and authors. It is unwise for the print buyer to assume that their suppliers understand all the legal issues involved in agreeing and executing a commission. The print buyer must therefore take steps to evaluate carefully all suppliers and to ensure that these suppliers understand all the legal implications and the ultimate uses of the job.

Warranties

Most content suppliers (including freelancers) accept the need to give warranties and indemnities. Some key authors, however, may refuse to enter into contracts that they consider onerous, while in other cases freelancers may convince the buyer of their suitability but may be unaware of the legal issues.

Warranties place on the supplier the requirement to observe the relevant laws affecting original materials. Most freelancers will be aware of what reasonable warranty clauses to accept. They must write in such a way as to say nothing that is libelous or injurious. Designers must be careful to ensure that the material used is not plagiarized from other sources. Without training or instruction, a designer or illustrator may do this unwittingly, but contrary to the terms of a warranty. For the print buyer the emphasis must be on careful selection, briefing and contracting.

In other warranty clauses, suppliers may seek to limit their responsibilities.

While the buyer must focus on careful selection of professional suppliers, the onus is on the supplier to make appropriate checks and obtain any necessary clearances within the agreed fee.

It is difficult for artists and designers working under pressure not to unintentionally copy the style of another artist or piece of work, or that of a previous publication. Other artists

Figure 2-3.
Example of a warranty
clause.

> The supplier hereby warrants that:
>
> 1. It is entitled to enter into this agreement
>
> 2. That the material is original and has not been used, sold or published previously
>
> 3. The material (e.g., the manuscript, publication, photograph, artwork or design) contains no libelous, defamatory, obscene or other unlawful matter and that it does not infringe the copyright nor violate any other right of any person, firm or company.
>
> The supplier hereby undertakes to indemnify the purchaser and its licensees against any loss, injury or damage (including legal costs) arising out of any breach of this warranty.

or competitors may argue that the material is being held out deliberately as their work for competitive advantage. Competitors will occasionally allege "passing off" in order to delay a competitive product or to reduce competition.

Where new material is being commissioned, the buyer will be wise to agree, and include in the contract, approval stages and dates for items like roughs, copy and final artwork. If there are disputes with the material submitted, the buyer must always write to confirm that the material is not acceptable, giving reasons, and explaining the next stage (e.g., resubmission).

Licensing

Licensing is the main alternative to the outright purchase of original material. Under licensing deals the buyer earns the right to reproduce specified material (such as a photograph or already published work) for an agreed use, time period, territory and medium. The payment will be based on a fee per period, per usage, or per copy produced. In some cases, payment will be made to the copyright holder in advance, in others following usage.

With the advent of digital text and images, computer networks and the Internet, licensing infringements (whether deliberate or accidental) are becoming more frequent. Publishers now permit the licensing of material from parts of existing works by larger customers who then customize the material, incorporate other licensed material, and in effect create a new work. An example of this is where universities license the use of material from a textbook, incorporate additional reading, customize the material with local prelims, and market the finished work to their students. It is anticipated that such licensing arrangements will become more common to an increasing number of customers.

Goods Title

Most work ordered by a print buyer is uniquely for the buyer's organization and has little resale value outside the contract. Paper and ink will have been expended to produce images and goods to the buyer's specification. The printer's standard conditions often refer to their right of lien over work that has not been paid for, although the printer will rarely have recourse to sell goods rejected by the buyer, in part because the printer has no copyright over the work.

Libel

Evaluating for libel, and libel disputes, are matters for specialized lawyers and libel attorneys, who will advise on problem copy. Nevertheless, large organizations with in-house lawyers still lose libel disputes. Some organizations will take the view that legal disputes over material that has been written about them will only serve as publicity. Others will feel slighted and will be driven to seek justice. One problem for the print buyer is that libel disputes, once referred to specialized lawyers, tend to create a certain momentum of their own, and the legal fees are in many cases higher than the damages.

3 The Supplier

Wilfried Wagner

Selecting the supplier is often seen as the most important decision a buyer is faced with, because the person who is asked to quote predetermines the quality of the end product, the service and the costs. You must at least know that the supplier has the necessary capabilities and experience to avoid wasting time and effort with a "no quote," or to find out later that your work has been passed on to someone else.

At best you will have a deliberate technique to assess your suppliers continuously and consistently. Although this may require extra resources on your part, the rewards are significant by keeping your business on a progressive and professional footing.

Importance of the Correct Supplier Base

To be able to respond effectively to the demands put upon you by your company, you need suppliers who are willing and able to work with strict procedural guidelines. At the same time it is desirable to aim to keep your input as uncomplicated as possible and in harmony with the industry's norms so that a great number of potential suppliers can be of service to you. Cost advantages can be achieved by tailoring your presentation of inputs to the requirements of the larger printers. You will gain better prices from cooperating with printers' own efficiency programs than from being known as a print buying prima donna.

Good suppliers have to be found and carefully developed. If circumstances prevent this, any possible shortcomings need to be identified before business is placed and contingencies planned for. In a normal business environment where a choice exists, a variety of suppliers should be established and maintained to ensure competition and provide adequate capacity for your needs. While some suppliers will be geared to high quality, technically challenging work, others should be able to handle simpler specifications cost-effectively.

Finding the Right Supplier

The first task is to determine what kind of supplier you need to get your work done. You will have made up your mind whether you want the whole job to be done by the printer or to source the origination elsewhere. The benefit of the latter approach is that you can choose the most suitable source for each discipline, but you will need to know which printing process will be employed and agree to some form of standardization for the proofing process and its control.

Printing processes. Printers tend to specialize by printing process. It is safe to say that the majority of printers specialize in sheetfed offset printing. Within this technology most companies — for reasons of their product and customer profile — limit available machine formats. Web offset printers, for example, specialize in long-run work of the kind that is suitable for their equipment and rarely stray into sheetfed offset except where necessary (for example, to print periodical covers). They may also limit their press sizes to eight or sixteen 8.5×11-in. (A4) pages for the same reason. Gravure printers tend not to employ offset at all (with a few exceptions).

As a consequence, specifications of the print you are buying may be so diverse that you need several types of printers to ensure that the most economical printing process and printing format is employed. An important part of your buying strategy should, therefore, be to identify how much you spend in each category and to ascertain that you have a sufficient number of suppliers for each, so that competition is maintained.

Research. Should you have to start from scratch, you will be examining your home market. What is of interest here is how much of the total production base in your category of purchase is potentially available for you to choose from, who these companies are and what their standing is within the industry. You may also want to know which companies are unlikely to be interested in your business because of their equipment or their contractual arrangements.

Trade directories can be of immense help. For example, the *Graphic Arts Blue Book*, published by A.F. Lewis & Co. Inc. of New York, lists companies and suppliers by region and specialty, often giving details of available equipment. Listings of this type, however, cannot be comprehensive or entirely up to date.

Like the aircraft industry, a handful of manufacturers equip the majority of companies of the graphic arts industry. If you are searching for a very specific process or piece of machinery, getting in touch with the manufacturers can be useful. You should be able to obtain names of companies and dates when the equipment was installed.

Word of mouth can be a promising approach. Asking colleagues in other companies for recommendations has the added advantage of giving clues about suppliers' attitude and first-hand practical experience.

There is something immensely professional attached to finding your suppliers rather than being found. More importantly, you may cut out the middleman.

Business cycles. Printers (and their banks) like little more than acquiring new machinery with the backing of a longer-term contract from a periodical customer. This contract will pay for the lion's share of the investment because it secures the major usage of the equipment in its initial years. It may also enable the shrewd print buyer to purchase excess capacity from a specialized printer at a discount. Periodical items include newspapers, magazines, travel brochures, mail order catalogs, and calendars.

Partnership sourcing. Government and business organizations in some countries (such as the United Kingdom) have been promoting this concept in recent years:

> "Partnership sourcing is a commitment by customers/ suppliers, regardless of size, to a long-term relationship based on clear mutually-agreed objectives to strive for world class capability and competitiveness."

If your requirements are complex and continuous then it is worth considering such an arrangement with your chosen supplier. The key benefit is to transform traditionally confrontational attitudes into teamwork based on openness and trust.

Partnerships are popular in Japan, but in addition print buyers in Japan have access to detailed independent price indexes, which provide the means to verify that what the supplier charges is indeed the promised bargain. The *Insatu Ryokin* (Printing Price Data) is published biannually by the Economy Research Foundation of Japan. This document contains a wide range of market prices, including, for example, prices of ink, printing plates, and paper. It is the lack of information in the West that makes the comparatively unimaginative "get three quotes" approach so appealing.

Innovation. Technical innovations in prepress, printing, and finishing processes can have a significant impact on the efficiency of your operation. It is therefore important for you to identify these developments and to lobby for progress. At least identify the innovators and stay in touch. Some examples of significant and relevant innovations in the recent past are set out in other chapters.

What to Look for in a New Supplier

A visit to a potential new supplier should be considered essential, and will be a most revealing experience. Not only will you find out how valued your business is but you should be able to get a feeling for the management style and how congenial internal working relationships are.

A checklist, prepared in advance, should assist you in this task. Besides the obvious things like the full address, whom to see and how to get there, the following checklist should be considered:

- Main purpose of business:
  - Product profile
  - Customer profile
- Future intentions:
  - Investments
  - Innovation
  - Location
- Management:
  - Ownership
  - History
  - Management tree
  - Turnover
  - Profit margin
- Employees:
  - Number employed (direct and indirect)
  - Industrial relations
  - Office working hours
  - Shifts
- Facilities and equipment:

- Plant layout
- Design and development
- Typesetting
- Reproduction
- Modem links
- Platemaking
- Printing
- Finishing
- Other services and specialities
- Warehousing
- Transport
- Overall impression
* Key materials used:
  - Plates
  - Inks
  - Paper
* Relationship with their suppliers
* Quality management:
  - Procedures
  - Accreditations
* Natural lead times
* Conclusions

References. Obtain the names of the potential supplier's ten most important customers. Select three and ask them for a reference. As well as general impressions, ask more specific questions that focus on your own requirements. You may want to create a basis for comparing one supplier against another by providing for the answers for each topic to be limited to "excellent," "good," "average," or "poor." You will be surprised how revealing the replies will be.

It is quite legitimate to ask the supplier for recent copies of the annual accounts. Also check your potential supplier's creditworthiness with a reference from Dunn & Bradstreet, Infocheck Ltd. or similar.

Similar work. Evidence of similar work already produced for other customers will be useful when considering the printer's ability to produce the work you need.

Competitive prices. You will need to prove early on that the supplier is competitive. The first stages of a new supplier's development should include costing exercises. Some judgment is needed over good prices — can these be maintained or are they an opening gambit? Are the prices low because the supplier operates on a shoestring budget and stands no chance of meeting your quality and service requirements? A cheap product that does not arrive is not a bargain.

Always ensure that prices are given in sufficient detail so that you are in a position to gain an insight into the relative efficiency of your supplier's operation and its purchasing power. The separation of fixed and variable cost by means of start-up cost and run cost, exclusive and inclusive of paper, ought to be the minimum you should know. This will enable you to cope with limited quantity changes and reprints without having to acquire another quote and assure you that changes in the price of paper are fairly applied. It will also provide you with useful pointers should price negotiations become indispensable.

Trial orders. Tests should be set up for any specialized processes that are identified as a risk. It may be prudent to place an initial order only. During the early stages of the cooperation the contact points should be broadened through various departments and levels of management. This is the best time to clearly define and obtain agreement to your requirements.

Induction. An orientation program for your supplier at your facilities is useful in case of day-to-day contact so that a good understanding is gained of your procedures and the reasons for them.

Supplier Management

A basic but essential requirement for dealing with your suppliers effectively is good and reliable communication. On balance over-communicating is called for, to avoid the many opportunities for misunderstandings in the habitually complex and unforgiving processes of the printing industry. The regret of not having over-communicated is strongest when you experience the numbing feeling which comes with having to destroy a production run because of a misunderstanding.

Aspects of Good Communication

The supplier should be instructed about the job to be done in clear, unambiguous terms. To do this you will need to have a grasp of the printing processes and their technical terms. If in doubt ask a printer to get involved in your planning stages. Having been at the receiving end for a long time, the printer is usually very experienced and more often than not will be able to make a useful contribution to design and specifications.

Instruct the supplier about procedures you wish to be followed. This can be in the form of a set of guidelines or a checklist, which should be kept up to date. Such guidelines should be discussed with the supplier and declared as part of your business terms and conditions. Try to keep them simple or you will pay extra. Topics would typically be:

- What details the quote should contain
- What constitutes placing an order with the supplier
- How, when and to whom to communicate progress
- Exception or routine reporting
- Technical requirements
- Proof and press approval procedures
- Quality control procedures
- Packing instructions
- Delivery instructions
- Invoice procedure
- Storage of plates and mountings

Keeping in touch. A supplier base is never static; poor suppliers improve, good ones can deteriorate, especially if neglected, and new ones need to be found. People change, both at the suppliers and within your company. They require a constant updating of procedural knowledge, awareness of strengths and weaknesses and the forging of relationships. This, together with the need to be aware of market conditions and new developments at and around your suppliers, cannot be done from behind the desk and over the telephone. A travel budget is necessary to keep in touch with your business.

Supplier evaluation. A formal evaluation document should be prepared annually for all your important suppliers, to be presented and discussed at a meeting between you and the supplier. The document should cover topics such as price, quality, service and prospects. The evaluation meeting is an opportunity to summarize the activities of the previous year and to agree how to move forward. A record of supplier performance over several years indicates whether the relationship moves in the desired direction.

To manage your suppliers effectively you will need statistics and measurements at hand. These typically include:

- Your worth to each supplier

- Your share of their total business
- What jobs they have from you
- Current and planned workloads
- Delivery, quality and service statistics
- Innovative contributions
- Who needs recognition and who requires special energy to improve

A simple point-scoring system may assist in identifying relative performance more precisely. An example is given in Table 3-1. Factors or weighting can be readily adjusted or expanded to reflect your priorities.

It is easy to spoil a good supplier by creating conditions that make it impossible to support you: too much business and you and the supplier may become dependent on each other. Too little business and you will lose the supplier's interest and not receive the best service when you need it the most.

Recognition. Some companies give recognition to their best suppliers by awarding certificates of business excellence. More practical recognition may come in the form of reduced inspection activity (quality certification), letters of encouragement, or more frequent opportunities to quote for work.

Improvement. Having identified your poorest performers leaves you with two choices — either to assist the supplier to resolve specific issues — this is best done by forming a team of experts from both sides, most concerned with the disciplines requiring improvement, or remove them from your list of approved suppliers.

Deletion. Resources may be wasted trying to improve a consistently poor performer over a long time. Deletion may require careful handling and dual sourcing to protect service.

Table 3-1.
Point-scoring system for evaluating supplier performance.

Factor	Performance (max. 100 points)	Weighting (total 100%)	Score
Quality of work done	90	40%	36.0
Price competitiveness	78	30%	23.4
Delivery record	80	20%	16.0
Relations	90	10%	9.0
Overall score			84.4

Obligations. If you are a major buyer you have a responsibility towards the industry which supplies you to identify and be vocal about its shortcomings and to provide cooperation and motivation to get improvements under way. This can also involve cooperation with manufacturers of equipment and materials and their research institutes.

Buying at Home or Away

There are, besides other considerations, sound environmental reasons why you should buy locally. On closer review you may find, however, that the materials your local printer is using have already travelled halfway around the globe. Suppliers that are not local may be more efficient in operation thus compensating for the extra time needed in transit by shorter lead times in production.

The printing industry is striving to develop and standardize data transmission and processing technology. This development will make printed results more predictable and location less of an issue.

There appears to be a psychological barrier, however, which prevents many buyers from considering a foreign country as a ready source of supply. The truth is that once you are inside a printing plant you can hardly tell which country you are in. Like airlines, printers all over the world operate the same machinery. But, in contrast to the airlines, prices do differ. The main reasons for this are differences in labor and material costs and exchange rates. The best way to break through the psychological barrier is to try it, and you may be in for a pleasant and profitable surprise.

When attempting to deal with foreign suppliers anticipate that it will initially take more of your time. If you cannot spare the time, do not start it. Mutual respect and trust are essential, but it is also imperative to tie up a tight legal contract. However, once signed, the contract should be put away. If you have to refer to it, something is wrong with the relationship. Keep the business simple: since you are to benefit from the cooperation you might as well help to make it a success. If your first language is English, your ability to converse with your foreign suppliers in their own language could be a courtesy that is appreciated, although it is likely that they speak some English anyway.

The single European market. The main purpose of the EU is to create an environment of non-discrimination between Member States. For the print buyer this has been largely achieved in the commercial sense: there appear to be no tariffs or subsidies or legislation that could favor or discriminate against a Member State.

The main benefit of the single European market is a stabilization of trading conditions which enables industries to compete through skill, innovation and investment; in other words, in ways that each supplier has control of. This, of course, implies stable exchange rates and, as long as they continue to vary, the print buyer has the opportunity for bargain hunting in Europe. European countries have been going through cycles of exchange rate movements that have enabled one country or another to offer lower prices for short or longer time periods.

Many countries maintain a Chamber of Commerce or a trade officer attached to their embassies in foreign countries, whose job it is to assist you in your inquiries. Trade organizations will be helpful in identifying suitable companies abroad. They will give you a general overview but may be reluctant to identify their member companies. Instead they tend to prefer to send your specifications to their members and let them approach you. This is probably not what you want.

There are, of course, trade directories as described earlier. Talking to equipment manufacturers or the editors of foreign trade magazines are alternative means of locating possible companies.

The short-term employment of a reputable, experienced industry expert as a consultant will get you the quickest results.

Supplier Relations

In general, the opinion that others have of your company is formed by their association and contacts with your employees. The buying department has a real opportunity and responsibility to enhance this reputation and the goodwill it commands.

In dealing with suppliers there are certain points of personal character and conduct that are requisites of a good purchasing professional.

Ethical codes may be determined by the company you work for, or may be written by some governing body (whether political or industrial); specific rules will vary from place to place. However, several basic tenets are universally applicable to all professionals when dealing with colleagues and suppliers, such as:

- Integrity
- Professional competence
- Complying with the law in letter and spirit

Some government and industry organizations (such as the Chartered Institute of Purchasing and Supply in the UK) offer guidance on the following subjects:
- Declaration of interest
- Confidentiality and accuracy of information
- Fair competition
- Business gifts
- Hospitality

On the subject of business gifts and hospitality, most agree that when it is not easy to decide between what is and is not acceptable, don't accept it. Another test is to accept only such considerations that you feel comfortable with and are in a position to reciprocate. If a business practice might reasonably be deemed improper, the best thing to do is reject it.

Summary

Time and energy spent on finding and managing suppliers must depend on the importance and the amount of print your business requires. If you have a major print job to handle once in a blue moon, you may be better off enlisting expert help for this occasion.

Try to keep your input simple and consistent with accepted practices. Measure your suppliers' performance, and keep statistics to encourage improvements in informed discussions. You are likely to gain keener prices and to find more suppliers who are willing to serve you.

Make it your business to determine which printing process is most economical for your specifications and ensure that your suppliers are equipped accordingly. There are many ways of discovering the right suppliers. Don't wait until they knock at your door. Go out and find them. Look at other countries as an extra dimension to competitive buying.

Good communications are vital to avoid mistakes which can end up being very costly. Support good communications by publishing guidelines for your general requirements as a reference for your suppliers.

4   Print Buying Developments

Chris Conolly-Smith

Introduction

Many observers have predicted the decline of paper-based products. In the twenty years since those forecasts were first made, paper-based products have grown in abundance. The overall volume of paper-based products, together with the variety of products printed on different substrates such as packaging, wallpaper, lottery tickets and direct mail, have all grown considerably. Emerging and newly developed countries are demanding more information and more sophisticated printed products and packaging as well as establishing new sources of printing for the international print buyer.

Multimedia and the Internet both offer new ways of reading and acquiring information, and of distributing that information from data source or publisher to the target reader. While young children and schoolchildren quickly embrace multimedia many will still demand information in a tangible form.

To the print buyer, new media technologies offer the opportunity to become a media buyer instead of just a print buyer, and in doing so become more useful to the organization. The reverse is also perhaps true, namely that experts or buyers of other media may depose the print buyer and reduce demand for those skills.

Technical or Organizational Revolution?

Organizational change has been as great as technical change. A print buyer cannot focus merely on technical updates, but must adapt to the changing and ever increasing demands of international competition, both for survival and growth. The print buyer must become accustomed to, and feel comfortable in, a rapidly changing business environ-ment. The success of a buyer is judged by the way he or she serves the needs of his or her organization. This does not, of course, preclude the buyer from using new techniques for competitive advantage, but not for technology's sake.

Industries are driven more by market factors than by their internal cost structures. This applies to the printing industry which must price according to the market and change accordingly, or enter new markets and specialities.

There has also been a growth in many countries of not-for-profit organizations such as charities and foundations. Many of these organizations are highly efficient and use the latest techniques in their operations as they seek to maximize surplus funds that can be applied to specific objectives and causes. New technology has also encouraged the emergence of numerous niche information providers.

The Modern Print Buyer

The increased competition and international nature of many businesses have forced organizations to change their definition of the right buyer for their firms. A buyer is now more often judged on the increased profit or value-added that is contributed to the organization. This concept is quite different than buying for the lowest cost per order. Many buyers work within, or report to, the head of a profit center rather than a cost center.

Many larger organizations will have a technical print adviser rather than buyer within a buying or services function. The adviser will then research new techniques and advise on color and technical standards issues such as formats or papers. In other organizations a specialized print unit may be responsible for generating films or disks for delivery to the printer. The emphasis in such organizations is on communication within the firm, with authors, picture agencies, designers and photographers, but not with printers. The negotiators and controllers will take advice from the technical specialist, although they will not necessarily act on such advice.

The head of the print purchasing unit has to possess strong commercial, control, communication, and management skills. These are outlined in greater detail below.

- **Commercial.** Negotiating skills; understanding how the organizations make a profit or surplus; understanding customer needs; understanding risk; analyzing estimates and invoices in a commercial rather than technical way; a basic understanding of economics; appreciating that time is money; understanding contractual and financial issues;

an awareness of the difference between the financial and the commercial.

- **Control.** Control through good planning of scheduling and technical elements, through motivating all the various parties involved, and through thorough research of suppliers and price trends, rather than acting merely as a technical controller.
- **Communication skills.** Good interpersonal skills; clear verbal and oral communication; good at meetings; an extrovert rather than an introverted, desk-bound specialist; an ability to explain and sell new projects to the suppliers and creative team; and a persuasive disposition.
- **Management skills.** A team player; having the confidence of, and in, colleagues; and motivational skills.

The above skills will be demanded from the head of the buying or print (or media) unit, and of those aspiring to that position in the future. These are skills required of managers rather than of experts. Within this unit the manager can have staff and resources for the technical elements. These will include: authors, designers and photographers; multimedia and electronics specialists; paper, printing and distribution specialists.

Depending on the size and specialized nature of the organization, these skills and resources may be achieved by in-house facilities, by freelance contract teams, or from advisers. While trends differ in different organizations and industries, the trend is towards freelance teams for each project. A project team might be appointed for the following:

- The introduction of a new packaging design
- An advertising campaign
- A book or book series
- Entry into the multimedia market

The Position of the Print Buyer within the Organization

Until 30 years ago a typical print buyer was found in the print production departments of magazine, newspaper, or book publishers. These departments would be staffed by former printers who had undergone their printing apprenticeships. Printed products were the main output of the organization, from which they obtained most of their revenue. However, the growth industries for printers have been the advertising, retailing and packaging industries. Here the printed products are part of the product mix, or a component of the organization's products (e.g., in packaging).

As printed products are not so dominant in such organizations, the role of the print buyer is different.

An example of likely future trends can be found among the large and powerful retailing groups which sell an ever increasing range of products. In such an organization there is someone who creates and organizes the production of a product. A fashion buyer, for example, will select the design and organize the manufacture of clothes items. The emphasis is on the creation and selection of marketable products suitable for sale within the retailer's outlets or by direct mail. In less specialized fields buyers move from one merchandise to another, which demands a different balance of skills and new technical knowledge.

Many such buyers are discouraged from becoming technical. The retail trade is fiercely competitive; margins are often tight, and profitability is achieved by volume or by reducing or eliminating working capital needs. Thus many of the latest buying and technical control trends originate from the retail trade. Examples of trends of this kind are:

- Objective, electronically-monitored color control standards
- The demand for faster, guaranteed deliveries in order to eliminate lost profit opportunities through out-of-stock situations
- Job pricing according to market rather than cost-plus estimating methods
- The change of printing management attitudes and marketing policies, and the introduction of electronic controls to reduce makeready times in order to make short runs economic (customers want only saleable products which they can sell quickly before demand trends change; storage areas have been converted into retail space)
- New invoicing and payment procedures; re-engineering of the total job from initial decision to the ultimate purchase by the retail customer
- New forms of negotiating and contracting for printed products; the supplier is sometimes asked to carry a stock or sales risk over a time period of several months.

Other examples of forward-thinking print buyers are motor manufacturing and software organizations. Both are global industries; accuracy is vital, and the markets are changing rapidly. There are many other examples. The trend is towards the professional buyer and commercial manager. Under the control of this manager may be three key sections:

- Design (creative activities and prepress)
- Production (printing, disc mastering and replication, and so on)
- Distribution (to customers, branches, stores and direct to the end user)

Production and distribution may sometimes be combined. In large units there may also be functional breakdowns as follows:
- Technical (including prepress)
- Purchasing
- Production control

Global or Local Purchasing?

There is no clear trend here although the majority of companies have chosen local purchasing within subsidiaries and divisions. The paper crisis over the period 1994–95 further encouraged group purchasing. For economies of scale, bulk discounts and priority scheduling can be achieved through centralized purchasing. Many organizations find that divisional purchasing departments working closely with creative and marketing departments are more motivated and have greater control, and thus achieve excellent prices and schedules. Where a large number of jobs are handled simultaneously and where printing and paper are not the larger part of a total budget, local purchasing is invariably preferred.

Supplier Relationships

In most countries market competition has led to a split between the printing and publishing functions. Few organizations combine both printing and publishing. Even some newspapers now subcontract the printing. This has led to lower costs of market entry and has resulted in several new newspapers and numerous new magazines. Organizations need to focus attention closely on the needs of their customers. Fast changing trends mean that demands on factory capacity levels and specialist machinery will alter. Within the same firm, publishing and printing divisions compete for capital and development projects. A need to replace printing equipment may cause market developments on the publishing side to be postponed.

In the past, many organizations have turned towards single sourcing, whereby suppliers were carefully examined and the best one selected for all or most of an organization's work. This made printers and their customers heavily interdependent. Such printers had, in effect, a monopoly on the customer's work, contrary to most generally accepted economic principles.

Many organizations continue to play the field, whether locally or worldwide. Print buyers have learned that cheaper estimates do not necessarily mean cheaper invoices for the total job, however. Large bureaucratic organizations continue to offer all work for tender. Each job is therefore viewed separately. An audit of all jobs produced in a year — viewed by format, type, finishing requirements, and the number of colors printed — would often suggest that better prices could be achieved by choosing a smaller number of specialized printers who understood the customer's needs.

The trend now is towards selecting a small number of favored specialist suppliers. Suppliers are sought on the basis of their specialized equipment and skills that match the needs of the customer. The suppliers work to prenegotiated price structures, are linked electronically with their customers, and understand their needs.

The emphasis is on the prompt identification of future print orders, the maintenance of adequate but low stock levels, and good communication between organizations at all levels. The needs of the accounting departments in both organizations will be taken into consideration. In particular, invoices will be submitted in a standard agreed form in order to reduce paperwork. In a print purchasing department this reduces the percentage of time that needs to be allocated to purchasing and invoice checking, and transfers the emphasis from administrative to managerial tasks. This gives an advantage to domestic printers who can often offer prompt service and excellent communication. Buyers may also select suppliers near their own end clients. Thus a North American publisher selling to the United Kingdom may favor a UK or European printer for delivery reasons.

New Technology

New technology is exciting; many buyers like to try out new technology for technology's sake. The key question for the buyer should be: what unique benefits and competitive advantage does the new technology give to me and my products?

In the fields of consumer electronics, new technology has rarely lasted for more than eight years before being replaced by a further development. Often the first printers to embrace new technology in a particular field have not thrived and have labored financially as a result. Many printers have chosen to wait. The exception has been where entrepreneurs with a clear understanding of the market and of marketing have purchased the new technology in order to give the customer a unique benefit.

Once established, the use of a new technology often creates an indispensable competitive advantage. In the case of the Xerox DocuTech, it has enabled marketing departments to produce prompt, focused or personalized mailings to target customers, thus leading to higher response rates.

Fierce international competition forced manufacturers to bring forward new advances and product innovations before users had fully exploited existing manufacturing resources using older technology. Examples of benefits from the new technology are:

- Computerized press controls:
  - More controlled color especially for reprints
  - More satisfied advertisers
  - Shorter start-up times
  - Reduced risk
  - The potential to hold lower stocks
- DTP:
  - Faster schedules
  - Greater control and flexibility
  - The ability to have concepts and mock-ups approved internally or by customers at low cost
  - More productive editors
- On-demand printing:
  - The ability to publish without holding stock
  - Lower stock risk and hence release of working capital
  - The ability to offer personalized individual mailings
  - Economic updating of topical publications
  - A lower cost of entry into publishing for entrepreneurs
- EDI:
  - Prompt delivery of information, orders, invoices, and payment
  - Transfer of digital information for decentralized printing, licensing, or sale
  - Improved price and control information

New technology offers, to designers and publishers, an infinite range of creative effects. Equally these same designers and publishers (or their advertisers) can make changes electronically at any stage in the process. A photographic image can be enhanced, or totally changed from the original shooting. While the aim is to continually improve the end product, the disciplined print buyer should surely insist, where appropriate, that improved planning prior to authorship and camera sessions will deliver a crisper, more effective publication or advertisement in a faster, more cost-effective way.

The Information Revolution

New media have a more attractive image than older, more mature paper-based products which are more price-sensitive. This is fast changing, as can be seen in the CD-ROM market where prices have fallen dramatically as the market has expanded and competition increased. Discs can be produced in small quantities with low-cost desktop equipment before mastering for long-run pressings. These offer the advantage of low-cost test marketing and on-demand production to the publisher, while offering high margins for a fashionable product to retailers on a fast turnaround. Nevertheless, it must be predicted that consumers will quickly become accustomed to CDs and welcome anew the separate advantages of the paper-based product.

Most analysts forecast a continuing (if different) future for paper-based products. In 1993 Mintel predicted a strong future for the book (the information book) because it is different to new technology and tangible. It is up to the print buyer to assist marketing specialists in designing new products and services that emphasize these advantages and differences, perhaps alongside electronic counterparts.

Some of the former command economies in Central Europe and states of the former USSR, and energetic Asian countries, have small or nonexistent paper and pulp industries. They will be vast potential users of paper as their market economies develop. Electronic products avoid the need for imports, or where suitable forests exist, the need to log these forests in a more environmentally aware world.

Market and Physical Distribution

New technology, however, blurs the differences in the roles of producer, publisher, and retailer. Convincing arguments can be made to suggest that the role of producer (the pressing of discs or similar products, or printing onto paper) can lie with the publisher or direct-marketer. If the product is distributed electronically, the retailer or the consumer can be responsible for production. Some record shops offer local cutting of CDs once the customer has previewed the product. Retailers could produce certain titles (such as out-of-print books) in-store, paying the publisher a license fee per disc or title sold.

Certain publishers already offer customized products to universities. These involve producing course-specific reading materials by combining elements of existing titles with the possible addition of new material.

The likely outcome is that printed products will follow the same route as TV companies whereby creative program production, distribution, and marketing functions are split into separate organizations. The program producer sells programs for once-only or repeat showing to TV companies (distributors) in different countries. This is very similar to coedition production and licensing in the book publishing industry.

Under this route the print production department may become the manager of an electronic and physical store of products and information. If published electronically, customers would have access to the database and pay a license fee as a member or per usage. The print production unit would be responsible for constant maintenance of this material in similar fashion to the way they have been responsible for maintaining film stores in the past. These archives will be major sources of future income to organizations.

This again reinforces the division of duties suggested earlier, namely design, production, and distribution.

In larger organizations not necessarily involved in print or media production, the trend is towards a logistics or distribution manager who coordinates and directs the total production, stock control, and distribution chain. Under this route the production unit would create products or services (like the TV production companies), and the logistics or marketing department would then be responsible for manufacture and distribution.

The production unit will have to possess a clear understanding of copyright and publishing law when contracting with authors, photo agencies, creative units and producers. Given that new technology allows the economic marketing of more and more niche products, this task will be immense and probably emerge as a separate role.

Fewer or More Standards?

Local standards have developed in different industries and in different continents. As a result, papermaking machines, sheetfed and web presses, binding and finishing equipment, envelope making and insertion machines may all be operated according to different standards.

Present and former centralized, command-led economies operate to rigorous single standards and thus are able to standardize on equipment specifications. When such economies become more market-led, producers start to use different formats for competitive advantage under a new-felt freedom from standards. In the U.S., the most market-led, most competitive economy in the world, most publications are to standard sizes. This gives economies of scale, and publishers achieve differentiation in the market by their content, design, or distribution rather than their physical size. New entrants to print purchasing work to the most common standards, e.g., the ISO A series (such as A4 and A5) in Europe. The A series is used for general printing purposes (such as publications) and includes sheet sizes based on a 33.1×46.8-inch (A0) standard sheet. Other sizes in the series (A2, A3, etc.) are equal to half the area of the preceding number (e.g., A1 measures 23.4×33.1 inches—half of A0).

Although adherence to standard formats can be seen as a constraint to creativity, the benefits (especially the reduction in wastage in comparison with nonstandard sizes) are considerable and in most cases the designer will be able to generate a satisfactory solution that emphasizes the USP (unique selling point) of the product or service without having to depart from the recommended sizes.

The increased power of the market and the consumer means also that standards must suit the demands of retailers and end-users. Thus mailings must fit standard envelopes within postal weight limits, must be compatible with inkjet personalized printing equipment, must be of a size to go through mail slots, and must lend themselves to email and Internet techniques in the future. Economic factors sometimes force the creation of new standards. Periods of inflation encourage customers to consider reducing the size and weight of their products in order to maintain existing prices.

Computer and electronic standards are being created regularly following the development of new technologies. The trend will inevitably continue and the buyer must take account of this fact. Most modern standards, while often seeking competitive advantages for the major manufacturers, take account of the upgrade path and compatibility. It may perhaps be difficult to select the ideal standard for a given purpose, but the consolation is that most standards will allow relatively simple, if inconvenient, transfer to future standards.

The Paperless Office

The paperless office has been prophesied for many years. Despite this prediction, the number of documents produced continues to rise and the photocopier remains the constant friend of office employees. Organizations involved in vast numbers of similar transactions have, however, moved in the direction of paperless records with some success, for example with document imaging systems or even voice recording replacing paper filing. Examples are stock exchanges and insurance companies. In many cases, office procedures have been reengineered to create a fundamental change of attitudes and procedures.

Print buyers constantly use the following documents and procedures:
- Request for estimate
- Estimate analysis
- Order preparation
- Scheduling preparation and control
- Delivery confirmation
- Payment approval

Other departments within the organization — the accounting department, the marketing department, the distribution depot — all exchange regular repetitive documentation with the production unit. With just-in-time (JIT) procedures increasing the number of smaller orders, more formal computer systems become essential.

The paperless office offers the following benefits to the organization:
- Accessibility of information
- Reduction in time spent on paperwork
- Analysis of costs per job, with easier estimate comparisons;
- Market price information (on a regularly updated database, using estimates received and other market information)
- The opportunity to incorporate cost/demand databases that are emerging on the Internet and on CD

The following benefits can be added through electronic document interchange (EDI) and networking within the organization:
- Electronic ordering and invoicing

- Faster estimates
- Faster turnaround

The paperless office is best introduced on a company-wide basis. This will involve a study of how the organization works, and will lead to a reengineering of certain procedures and individual roles. Thus the print production role would be viewed as part of the total organization and value chain. This inevitably involves change and perhaps fear of job losses. Organizations that have many years of experience in the information industry with paper-based products would do well to visit or study young organizations that have entered the field, and observe their attention to niche markets. All decisions are customer- or market-led, and the emphasis is on satisfying the customer. Most of the staff are employed to study and cater to customers' existing and future needs, rather than dealing with production issues. Young, new organizations of this kind, enabled and encouraged by new technologies, are springing up worldwide and often quickly become competitors in niche areas.

The organization needs the same skills and qualities already advocated here for media managers and those aspiring to that position: a market-aware, commercial, computer-confident manager with strong communication skills. To the joy of seeing creative ideas develop from concept to printed page can be added an even more exciting challenge involving sound and moving images in a convergence of many different media. The print buyer may need to fight to retain that role, at least in its entirety.

This chapter has been about development, but many of the concepts discussed are already in action. The drive for increased profitability through innovation and efficiency cannot be avoided.

5 Briefing

Deborah Kamofsky

A brief describes and defines a commissioned task. In the context of buying design and print, the brief can (in its most comprehensive form) define commercial and contractual context as well as the procedures and outcomes of a design or a print commission.

The need for a brief assumes the requirement to subcontract or delegate some or all of the processes required to produce a finished product.

Subcontracting is the commissioning, usually for payment, of resources outside those available within your organization in order to produce a product or supply a service that meets your organization's needs. Your goal as the commissioner remains the fulfillment of a specified outcome, to an acceptable quality, within time and cost limits.

The potential benefit of subcontracting is that it enables you to buy into greater resources in skill, time or equipment than you have in-house. The potential disadvantage is that the external subcontractor will produce according to its own capability and viewpoint. It may know nothing of your organization's mission or ethos and be unfamiliar with the language, style, and visual personality which represent it.

If delegating work within your own organization (where it is more likely that capability is known and viewpoints shared) you may still find it beneficial to generate a clear set of instructions to facilitate and direct.

The brief for the design and production phases of a product have quite different requirements, since the one is focused on creatively exploring the possible ways of meeting the requirement (through as many iterations as are needed), while the production brief is more a set of instructions aimed at realizing the product described by the design process.

The Design Brief A design brief can be used to select, inform and create contractual agreements between the commissioner and supplier of creative services. These services are focused around the design stage of the print production process, and may also include copywriting, illustration and photography.

The product is most often a piece of printed material, but increasingly involves digital media such as an interactive CD or a Web site. Whatever form it takes, the way in which information is presented — its visual format and aesthetic suitability — will still, to a large extent, determine its effectiveness.

The designer's role at the creative stage of a project is to help the client to plan and construct a product which will effectively communicate the client's desired message to its chosen market. As well as providing background to enable the designer to understand the nature of your organization, the brief should describe an outcome and provide a structured contractual framework.

A designer will often take responsibility for the other contributors to the design process. The greater the designer's scope, the more critical the brief becomes, as more of the creative responsibility is allocated to a single subcontractor.

Many designers will be prepared to manage the print production part of the process; if knowledge of print is adequate, the designer can be an effective bridge between the creative input and the production processes.

The Print Production Brief The print production brief can be used to select, brief and create a contractual agreement between the commissioner and the supplier of printing services. It should enable a match of the requirements of the product to the capabilities of the production process to obtain the maximum value at the lowest possible cost.

Its function is initially to estimate and compare cost, in order to select a printer. It can then develop, through discussion, to define a product in sufficient detail to ensure that the finished product meets the needs of the client and observes the requirements of the production processes.

Lastly, its function is contractual: it defines what will be supplied when, how and at what cost.

The purpose of a brief. It is impossible to guarantee that a subcontractor will be able to produce the result that you want. How then do you minimize the risk and prevent a potential waste of time and money? You must find a way to communicate your needs to someone who you believe may be able to supply the appropriate service or product, at the right time, to an appropriate quality, and at an appropriate price.

From the mundane simplicities of quantity and schedule to the vague subjectivity of aesthetic judgment — a brief provides a framework for development, specification, evaluation and negotiation.

Good design is fundamental to the way your product is received. A designer's role can be seen as that of a translator: it is the designer's responsibility to listen to the objectives and values expressed by the client, interpret them and translate them into a visual representation. The clearer and more focused the brief, the more quickly a designer will arrive at an apt solution. It is very difficult to convey images with words, and it is not easy to articulate a visual solution to an intellectual problem. As a client your role is to be as clear and objective as possible. This should enable a design professional to arrive at an appropriate solution.

Design involves emotion, aesthetics and fashion as well as straightforward information. Reducing the potential for prejudgment and subjectivity enables a designer to focus on the best solution for your organization and your market. You don't have to like it — it has to work. Judging that you have arrived at the agreed design outcome can be a subjective and difficult process, and the brief (which incorporates approval/proceed points) enables each stage to proceed with assent. At each stage, the commissioner agrees with the creative supplier that the project is moving in the agreed direction.

Because the outcome is a product, the print brief describes a more tangible, more objectively measurable output. The brief or specification for print is required to be a literal set of instructions rather than a contextualized goal. It describes in detail the structure of a printed piece and provides a basis to determine whether a client has, or has not, received the goods described.

Both the design brief and the print brief act as an aid to clarifying the contract between the purchaser and supplier by defining the following aspects:
• The product
• The market
• The budget
• The schedule
• The amount and schedule of payment

Briefing a Designer

A clear design brief can facilitate the initial selection of a designer; the development and then the unambiguous specification of your visual solution; and the clarification of the contractual basis of the purchase.

It serves a different purpose at each stage of the process and should develop and become more focused as the project progresses, serving as a catalyst to selection, creativity and contract. Thus the stages in the design process are:

1. Selection
2. Visualization
3. Production
4. Evaluation and approval

The nature and purpose of each stage will be considered in turn.

Selection

You may know exactly what you want to produce, or you may just be aware of the goal that you aim to achieve. You need to select a designer that is able to translate your wishes into an effective visual product at a suitable price, within your time frame.

Construct a brief that highlights your key goals and use it to clarify the purpose of the final product. As well as encouraging you to be clear about your aims and objectives, it will also enable a designer to consider your needs and evaluate their own ability to meet them.

The brief at this point is open. It describes context and outcome but not process. You are indicating the skills and experience needed to complete the brief, and you are aiming to attract a designer able to:

- Accurately represent your organization
- Visually interpret your organization's mission
- Reach the target market in an appropriate style
- Meet your schedule
- Meet your budget constraints
- Generate a design that can be produced efficiently

Your brief should provide information and provoke questions. Among other things, it should include:

- The goal
- Background information about your organization
- The time frame for completion
- The parts of the process for which you will be responsible

- The areas for which you expect the designer to take responsibility
- The budget parameters

Once you have some responses to your original brief, you could arrange a meeting with each potential designer. Alternatively, you could prepare a short list with a competitive pitch for the work with initial visualizations, in order to help you make a final selection on the basis of a designer's approach to your actual problem. To select in this way you need either a budget to pay for the initial visuals, or an attractive enough project to encourage an unpaid (free) pitch. This could possibly work to your disadvantage by excluding smaller design groups who cannot afford to pitch unpaid and, ironically, may be best able to meet your requirements economically.

Design fees vary greatly, and relative cost and value are often difficult to predict and compare. Focusing on the designer's ability to solve your problem for your organization removes some of the subjectivity which can affect selection.

When considering designers, it is important that you like their work, that you can communicate with them, and that you can see that they have solved similar design problems before. It is also pertinent that they can subjugate their own visual preferences to achieve the goals of the design.

It is even more important that the designer can demonstrate an understanding of the nature of your requirements, and is prepared to accept the brief in your terms. This acceptance is the first contractual stage: understanding the task, demonstrating that they are equal to it, and accepting the brief.

Of course, if you have already worked with a designer before, you will already know the answers to some of these questions and the briefing process will be less rigorous.

The design of a visual communication cannot exist independently of the medium, and a large part of the designer's role is to reconcile the requirements of the product with the process of reproducing it. Although a good design is a creative solution to the problem identified by the brief, the designer should also have sufficient technical knowledge of production. The designer who understands print process capabilities will be better able to deliver value through the production chain to the final product.

Visualization

Once you have made your choice, your contractual relationship begins, and the brief will start to become more focused in order to facilitate the translation of that goal to word and image. Three areas need to be clearly described and agreed upon:

- The goal of the product
- The context (your organization and the market)
- The contractual parameters

The goal of the project should as far as possible be articulated in terms of clear objectives, defining the message that you are trying to communicate. To do this you may need to describe the change in behavior that you are trying to achieve, the benefits that you want to convey, and the response that you want to generate.

You may have some idea of the form that the message will take: how you visualize the final product, what medium it will use, and what other literature or stationery it will need to be compatible with.

Through an awareness of the contextual framework of the message that you are trying to convey, the designer will be able to develop an appropriate visual language with which to convey it. This context will include information about:

- Your organization
- Your target market
- The competition

You should help the designer understand your organization by briefly describing its background and mission, and giving information about its mix of products, markets and services that distinguish it from its competitors. Any existing corporate identity should be carefully explained, preferably by supplying corporate guidelines if they exist or examples of previous work.

To define your target market, you will need to explain who the message is aimed at, and give as much information as possible about demographic and social profile (e.g., age, sex, social class, location, occupation, status, financial position, personal values and interests). It will also be helpful if you have an understanding of their visual culture and a knowledge of their reading habits.

The competition can be described in terms of the other organizations in the same market, their products, and their strengths and weaknesses in comparison with those of your own organization.

Production

At the production stage in the design process, the designer will undertake a range of activities that are necessary to fulfill the creative concept agreed earlier. The brief should describe the proposed outcome of the project, and the contractual parameters surrounding its supply — not just in terms of cost, but including all elements of the exchange.

The larger and more complex the project, the more important it is to detail the individual processes involved in the production of a finished design, and the likely costs that will be incurred for each. Items that may be covered in the brief include:

- Researching the project (including meetings, market research and testing)
- Design development (working up concepts and visuals)
- Content preparation (copywriting and editing, photography, picture research, and illustrations)
- Page assembly (page make-up, layout proofs, author's corrections)
- Prepress production (bromide or film output, scanning, film output, color proofs)
- Print production (printing, finishing, and delivery or distribution)
- Expenses (phone calls, travel, couriers, materials)

Each of these items can be included in the brief and can have separate costs attached. Harder to quantify in this way, but no less important, is the quality of the finished design. While you may not be able to contract specifically for good design, you can set criteria (such as implementing corporate guidelines, or following the guidelines for artwork preparation covered in Chapter 7). It is also possible to link part of the fee to the achievement of these criteria, if you can demonstrate that you apply such criteria consistently.

Of course, you cannot contract for liking the final result, nor should you need to as long as the finished result works in terms of the brief that you have agreed to.

Evaluation and Approval

What happens if you do not like the first visuals? What happens if the photographer is late? You will reduce the risk of conflict if basic issues like this are considered in the contract. Far from being threatened by the inclusion of such contingencies in the contract, an experienced designer is likely to be pleased that you are able to deal with them in a professional way.

The contract with the designer should cover the following details:

- What the designer is responsible for
- What they will in turn subcontract to other suppliers
- The basis of charges
- Lines of responsibility (who will be responsible for what decisions)
- Contact details (how people can be reached)
- The approval cycle
- The production schedule
- The budget and any changes in the projected cost
- The payment schedule
- Provision for contingencies
- Legal issues such as ownership of copyright

The details of the contract should be embodied in a standard document rather than rewritten for every project. Only larger projects with unique features will need a contract to be written from scratch.

Briefing the Printer

While the design brief will normally evolve through several iterations, the brief to the printer is usually more stable and acts as a specification that clearly defines the inputs and required outcomes of the process.

A specification is, according to ISO 8402, "The document that prescribes the requirements with which the product or service has to conform." A successful brief to the printer will enable the description and unambiguous specification of the printed product. It should also describe the contractual context surrounding the production and supply of goods.

As with the design brief, it will start as an open description with options, and become more specific as it develops into a closed contract.

The more detailed and accurate your print specification, the better your printer's chance of preparing an accurate costing and the better the chance that the end product will match your goals.

The stages in developing the print specification (each considered in turn below) are:

1. Selection
2. Product development

3. Production
4. Evaluation and approval

Selection

You may find it beneficial to select a printer early in the design process so that both printer and designer can participate in the development of the brief. A strong partnership between designer and printer is more likely to result in an effective printed product.

The goals at this stage are:
• To estimate the cost of the prospective product
• To enable comparison of suppliers and the selection of the most appropriate according to the specification, budget, quality expectation, quantity and schedule
• To explore the implications of variations to the specification and consider options that may add value to the design, or may enable it to be produced more efficiently
• To create a basis for negotiation

Your aim is to communicate your desired end product as quickly and clearly as possible. The key to specifying is familiarity with the language. The language of print is riddled with technical jargon, abbreviations and vernacular expressions. To add complexity, this language is often applied inconsistently and therefore relies heavily on common understanding and context.

A common understanding can be based on this language, but even within the trade, discrepancies occur. It is usually better to describe the desired outcome than to specify a precise process or method, if you have any doubts whatsoever that your description is open to interpretation. If you are unclear about any part of the specification, supply a visual representation of it instead of a textual one — draw it or do a mock up and send that to the printer. Many buyers feel that if they do not appear to be completely well-versed in the technical terminology, it lessens their buying power. Avoid using jargon in an attempt to exert control, as the resulting errors or ambiguities often have the opposite effect.

Try to present your description in the sequence which most quickly draws the picture and makes sense. In order to make sure you are comparing like with like, present the information in an identical way to each printer you are considering. Ask for separate costs where options may change. It is essential to identify these options clearly, rather than forcing the printer to search for them.

Cost Breaks

Several printers may be approached. As their capabilities may be different, the brief should be open enough at this point to allow each printer to let you know where they can offer the best value. The size and capabilities of the equipment will tend to either constrain or enable changes in the specification. Unless you know these parameters well, ask questions that allow the printer to reveal them.

For example, a printer with a 19×25-in. press may be able to offer a nonstandard page size at lower additional cost than a printer with a 25×38-in. press. Similarly, a printer with in-house die-cutting may be able to offer the addition of a die-cut pocket more economically than one who has to subcontract the work to a trade finisher; and a printer with a five- or six-color press will be able to offer an extra color or a sealer varnish more economically than one with just four-color machines.

Ask open questions to elicit ideas from the printer. At this point, asking rather than specifying can offer the greatest scope for economy. Each time you request an estimate you will discover more about your printers and their capabilities. Solicit ideas to enable printers to demonstrate their scope and show where cost breaks fall. You will also get a sense of how much the printer is prepared to support you with creative and technical advice.

Encourage cost presentation in a form that enables comparison. The brief should be structured to enable clear comparison between printers. Work from a clear base product option and request variations from appropriate points.

You may choose to devise a form that lets each printer write costs against headings that you have selected. This will ensure consistency in the presentation of costings, and should ensure that there are no unexpected consequences arising from the particular word choice used by the printer.

The Print Specification

Every product will have a different specification, and standard specification documents are only useful in organizations where the work is highly repetitive. However, there are some basic factors that should always be taken into account when preparing the specification.

Reference information. Help the printer to identify your job by giving it a brief working title and description. Supply your own reference for the job, if any.

Description. A description of the purpose of the job is very helpful for the printer. This should be included in addition to the essential information on quantity, run on, finished size, flat size if relevant (the unfolded size of a single sheet item), the number of pages, the number of colors, and the paper or board to be used. Make sure that you give separate details for the cover, including any gatefolds or other requirements.

When specifying the paper or board to be used, you can either give the merchant or mill brand name, or describe it generically with a qualitative guideline (e.g., 170 gsm gloss art — Ideal Premier or similar). At the stage when you are selecting a printer, the specification should preferably include a brand name so that you have a genuine comparison between prices, but ask for their recommendations as well so you can benefit from any special deals that they have with their merchants.

Make sure that you give full details of the finishing requirements. If the product has unusual finishing requirements, a dummy of some kind is essential for the printer to visualize the effect that you want to achieve.

In order to explore the possible options on sizes, colors, number of pages and run lengths, ask the printer to give you the economic steps. For example, if the printer runs a 25×38-in. press, it will print sixteen 8.5×11-in. pages on a single sheet, so 32 pages will be substantially cheaper than 36 pages, and quite possibly cheaper than 24 or 28 pages.

Prepress. Make clear exactly how you will supply the origination materials to the printer, and what stages you expect him/her to carry out. For work to be supplied on disk, identify the hardware platform (e.g., Mac or PC) and software used (e.g., PageMaker, QuarkXPress, Illustrator, etc.) to create the files. For pictures, give details of the number of originals and their final output sizes, and clarify whether you are supplying any high-resolution files and whether the printer is required to color-separate them.

Approval. List the approval stages and the type of proofs you want. Consider whether you need multiple proofs so that you can send copies to different departments within your organization, or retain them for internal records.

The context of the individual job should also be addressed, either through the specification itself or through supporting information. The kind of details that the printer will find useful include:

- Whether the specification is final or likely to change
- Whether the job is a one-off, or part of a series that it must conform to in details such as paper or special colors
- Whether any special production capabilities are required
- Whether the product will need to be updated in the future
- What kind of price is sought — a budget in which all eventualities are covered, or a competitive pitch
- Any special requirements for the product, and any items of critical importance (such as a book that must lay flat when opened, or a corporate identity color that must be matched)
- The proposed schedule, including the time of year, whether deadlines are "no fail" or merely preferred dates, and the time you will need to return the proofs

Discuss, if you can, the cost structure that will be applied to corrections. If the schedule is likely to require overtime work, clarify the additional costs related to each process, as the amounts involved are likely to be different at different stages of production.

Product Development

As the product is designed, the specification will change. Respecify to adjust your initial specification if necessary. A small change to the design can sometimes have a radical effect on cost or product integrity. You may need to adjust items such as finishing style, finished size, pocket sizes or color configuration according to what is economic and effective. If your company is subject to value-added taxes (VAT), you may also want to explore the implications of the new specification for VAT liability, since for some products adjusting the specification could change their exemption status.

Production

The specification for production is of course very similar to the brief for estimating, but without options. Many estimates are phoned in to printers, and if the printer confirms the estimate in writing you have an opportunity to check that the specification is as intended. When you place a job with the printer, however, it is essential that the specification is confirmed in writing. Any subsequent revisions or additional instructions should also be confirmed in writing (even if initially given by phone). This minimizes the chance that your instructions will be overlooked, and puts you in a stronger position in the event of a dispute.

Details such as run length (including requirements for minimum quantities and overs), schedules, and any references need to be confirmed in the specification and qualified as necessary.

Evaluation and Approval

In broad terms, the print specification defines the agreement between the printer and the purchaser, and forms part of the contract between them.

An approval cycle based on agreed time frames, procedure points and payment terms protects both parties. The approval stages should be clarified, and it should be agreed whether the job will need to be passed on press.

The specification should also incorporate any quality standards that apply to the finished product. Published standards (such as those referred to in Chapter 8) incorporate procedures for measuring quality parameters and appropriate tolerances, but for other criteria you will need to give details. For example, if you want to specify the permitted variation in a special color, you should either give colorimetric values and tolerances or supply printed examples that illustrate the range of color variation that is acceptable.

Background Issues

The briefing stream drives both creative and production processes by defining the key elements in the production of a printed product. It clarifies the purpose of the product, maps out the budget and schedule for production, describes how the different stages will be controlled and evaluated, and defines the end product itself.

A successful brief clearly instructs a subcontractor to fulfill a creative or practical project in exchange for payment. On a simple level a brief defines goals and parameters. On a more complex level, it formalizes language and communication structures and forms a basis for development and completion outside subjective language.

The written brief can only support and structure the exchange of creative services for money. If there is no common understanding of the goal, the project will still leave the client feeling that they have not bought what they wanted.

Language and Knowledge

The brief forces a client to take responsibility for placing instructions to produce a product that the client may not fully understands, but nonetheless must agree to buy. For this reason, much of the role of the designer and printer is to explain and clarify the product that they have agreed to sell. Without understanding, the contract is empty. It is also the reason why the more inexperienced a client is, the more one should focus on the outcome of the process, rather than the process itself.

To be effective the briefing stream requires the existence or development of an agreed language and terminology to facilitate communication, remove ambiguity and to allow an agreement to be reached.

Relationship

You will set the scene with your initial inquiry. The very way in which you make this inquiry will determine the printer's view of your product. As well as trying to understand the product you plan to produce, the printer is also making a judgment about you. Do you know what you are talking about? Do you have a realistic idea of the nature of the process? Will you be honorable as a client? Have you got a sense of humor?

Remember that when you begin to select a printer, the printer is also making decisions about whether to choose you as a partner!

Framework

In addition to simple language, the brief also operates within a context where standing instructions are implied even if unstated. These are tacit areas of specification which could be general cultural customs or specific production habits that have developed during a working relationship. They may not be recorded as part of a formal contract but will still be deemed by the client as part of the implicit communication.

For example, a client may work a particular daily routine so that "first thing in the morning" is considered to be 10:00 am and "close of play" is 7:00 pm. These daily deadlines overlay any schedule agreements, but may not appear in the written specification.

A clear agreement regarding contractual obligations on the part of both customer and supplier is essential. Otherwise the working relationship can become a frustrating and time-consuming negotiation over money or schedule, rather than a partnership to maximize creative productivity.

The briefing process requires a respect for approval procedures, and an understanding of their role in the contract. This will, of course, never eliminate the possibility of argument: for example, if a typo has been set by the designer and the client has failed to notice it through several sets of proofs and the error appears in the finished product, the client will still feel that the designer is to some extent responsible for the error. In these situations you have to find a way to agree in whatever way you can, preferably in good faith and with a commitment to learn from the process. The designer will be right to reject responsibility for this error, but could lose the client's goodwill and possibly even future business as a result.

If a printer reprints a product and your initial brief specified a matte art paper, the printer could conceivably print on a different matte art paper from the initial run. The printer would have fulfilled the brief, but you may be annoyed that the paper is not identical — you might assume that this is a standing instruction. A balance must be found between writing everything down so that you are contractually faultless, and making sure that your needs are understood and respected, which is not the same thing. Moreover, excessive detail in a specification makes it likely that it will not be read fully, and that significant items may be lost among the trivial details.

The brief works alongside any background information the designer or printer already has. As they work with you over a period of time, they will build up a level of understanding of your organization and your personal preferences and will add this knowledge to your brief. A good supplier will confirm assumptions: the supplier may be wrong in a given instance, but equally the writer of the brief may omit essential details as the supplier demonstrates an increasing understanding of the client's needs.

With good communication based on established relationships, the working relationship between the client and the designer becomes clearer and it is then easier to design products that accomplish their desired objective.

Complicated by its own vocabulary and language, riddled with the vernacular and often masked by idiom, communication about design and print can be problematic at best. Add the element of subjectivity in evaluating design value and print quality, and the situation can become a minefield, so:

- Speak in an agreed-upon language
- Prioritize what is meant over what is said
- Bear in mind the legal context hidden in the small print
- Always retain your sense of humor

This is the best route to consensus.

6 Materials

Phil Green

This chapter aims to assist you in maximizing the value you obtain from the materials used in the manufacture of printed products, by giving guidance on the selection of paper and inks and an awareness of contemporary production methods and the materials available.

Paper

Paper is made from cellulose fibers that have been treated and mixed with additives and a large volume of water. This "stock" flows onto a moving wire mesh where much of the water drains away, leaving a continuous mat of fiber which then passes through pressing and drying rolls to be eventually wound up as a reel of dry paper. On the way through the papermaking machine it will receive surface treatments such as size (a waterproofing agent), coating, and calendering, depending on the nature of the type of paper being produced.

Pulp and paper manufacture are global industries, and a number of trends in manufacture and distribution affect the availability and price of paper. These trends are underpinned by a continuing rise in worldwide demand for paper, which is forecast to continue and indeed accelerate, particularly as literacy grows in the Far East. Increasing demand for paper makes continual investment in new papermaking capacity necessary.

For standard papers, such as newsprint and publication grades, the rise in volume has encouraged the formation of large multinational concerns that often control the whole of the production and distribution chain, from the source of raw cellulose fiber (the forests and pulp mills) to the sellers of finished reels and sheets (the mill agents and paper merchants). Smaller mills are unable to reach the economies of scale for standard grades, and tend to produce mainly specialized grades such as cover papers or even small quantities of bespoke products.

The raw cellulose fiber used in papermaking, known as pulp, is produced mainly from northern hemisphere conifers. The steady rise in demand for paper and other wood products has put pressure on the forestry industry, and the rise in pulp prices has forced papermakers to consider alternative fiber sources. Since paper is readily made from almost any cellulose fiber, there are many alternatives including the bulky residues of other agricultural crops such as straw and bagasse (a waste product of the extraction of sugar from sugar cane) and fast-growing plants such as esparto grass and hemp. Purpose-built mills that utilize these types of fiber are likely to multiply in the not-too-distant future.

There are many other trends in the manufacture and distribution of paper that can be identified.

Back selling is the name given to the increasing effort that paper merchants are making to target the specifier of paper (the print buyer and designer in particular) for their sales and promotion activities, bypassing the printer who has traditionally been the one to deal with the merchant.

Alongside this has been the development in improved customer relations, notably in making information more readily available and providing technical support and alternative ordering and payment methods.

Papermakers have greatly improved the consistency of finished paper through the introduction of sophisticated quality controls, both to reduce waste levels and to protect themselves against the claims for substantial losses that can occur when substandard paper is supplied.

The increasing demand for color in all types of printed product has led to a range of better surfaces becoming available on lower grade papers. Two prime examples of this are the light-weight coateds now used in many periodicals, and the improved newsprint used in publications such as weekly newspaper supplements.

Coating methods have been the focus of extensive research, and new on-machine coatings such as film coatings have been developed, again mainly for the lower grades of paper.

Finally, there has been an increase in concern over the environmental impact of paper, and the forestry and papermaking industries have found themselves having to respond to both consumer and legislative pressures.

Paper and the Environment

Print buyers are increasingly expected to consider environmental issues in producing a printed product. Although a focus on the environmental consequences of print materials can seem to be a costly and unnecessary activity, it can have real benefits in waste reduction and a better public perception of the purchasing organization.

Environmental concern has focused on three major stages in the life of paper products: forestry, papermaking, and the eventual disposal of the finished product. (The printing processes have also come under scrutiny, with much attention focused around solvents in inks and fountain solutions. That, however, is a subject too great to be discussed at length here, and is the topic for another book.)

A major anxiety for environmentalists in recent years has been the loss of tropical rain forests. In fact very little pulp is sourced from these regions, although there are some exceptions such as:

- The logging of the Amazon region in Brazil to make way for Eucalyptus plantations
- The use of tropical hardwoods in the growing pulp and papermaking industries of developing countries like Indonesia

In the northern-hemisphere countries where most pulp is produced (particularly North America and Scandinavia), timber may come either from primary forest (also known as old-growth or virgin forest) or from farms. Logging of primary forest results in loss of habitat for native plant and animal species (a major concern since population size is usually strongly related to habitat area, and some species are seriously endangered as a direct result of this loss), and can lead to serious erosion damage if clearcutting practices are adopted.

Farms pose less of a threat to the environment, although heavy use of agricultural chemicals and soil erosion take place if forests are managed poorly, and there tends to be a reduction in habitat quality. Generally the pace of growth of secondary forests is not sufficient to keep pace with the rising demand for pulp, and as a result there has been an increase in pressure on the primary forests.

In discussing the environmental impact of the pulp industry it is important to recognize that paper pulp is not the sole product of forestry, and indeed it often uses the by-products of other industries such as furniture-making, or thinnings from growing trees.

Pulp and papermaking have in the past been a major contributor to the pollution of waterways, through the discharge of wastes containing large quantities of minerals and chemicals, including chlorine compounds and trace amounts of dioxins from bleaching processes. Treatment of wastewater is now compulsory in North America and Europe, and dioxins have to some extent been eliminated by moving away from chlorine bleaching (mainly substituting hydrogen peroxide as the bleaching agent). Wastepaper is disposed of in three principal ways:
• Incineration
• Landfill
• Recycling

Modern incineration plants can be a major source of energy, although there are emissions of carbon dioxide (a greenhouse gas that contributes to the process of global warming).

Landfill can also provide a source of energy by harnessing the methane vapors released. The lack of suitable sites is making landfill an increasingly costly option.

Recycling is the most efficient method of disposal, but it requires substantial investment in collection and treatment. Wastepaper has to be deinked and repulped, and the cellulose fibers need to undergo a restoration process to make them suitable for papermaking again. Recycled fiber that is made into the lower grades of paper requires less treatment and it is more efficient to down-cycle paper rather than use it for premium grades, although the treatment plants built by some papermakers are capable of producing sheets every bit as good as those made entirely from virgin fiber.

The environmental impact of paper should be viewed in terms of the key issues of energy use, pollutants, habitat, and the carbon cycle. Where possible environmental audits and life cycle analyses should be used, rather than relying on simple solutions such as increasing the demand for the use of recycled fibers in every type of printed product. A variety of labeling systems are in use that attempt to rate the environmental impact of different papers, although some labels can be ambiguous or even misleading. Currently the European paper merchants federation is attempting to create a stan-

dard label that can be used by all paper suppliers to provide
product information in a consistent way.

**Paper and Board
Selection**
The choice of paper or board makes a fundamental contribution to the effectiveness of a printed piece, and has a key role
in the value that the end product has to the immediate client
and to the end-user.

To make the right choice of paper the specifier must carefully analyze the purpose of the printed communication: the
message and its intended audience. Does it have a purely
functional role, or is it important to convey aspects of the
organization's image? Is it primarily an internal communication, or will it be seen by customers? Should the paper
simply support the message, or should it attempt to enhance
it? Is paper the right medium for the message, or would it be
better conveyed on an interactive medium such as a CD or on
the Internet? How do the tactile and appearance qualities of
paper contribute to the communication?

Depending on the intended audience, choosing a high-
quality paper does not always support the message. For
example, an unusual and expensive paper may convey
sophistication and prestige to some recipients, but may
induce anxiety in others, especially if the cost is seen as
inappropriate.

Paper should ideally be chosen at an early stage in the
design process, as it will affect other choices that may be
made, such as the type of images that can be successful on it.
As well as the usual merchant swatch books, the specifier
should have access to a range of printed samples of work, as
this can demonstrate what works better than blank samples.
Paper seems more rigid in smaller sizes, so it can be misleading to choose papers from swatches. Many larger merchants
provide an excellent sample service to paper specifiers, and
will happily make up dummies in the size of your finished
job at short notice.

The aim of the paper specifier should be to choose a paper
that meets the design brief and optimally supports the
intended message, but also contributes to the efficiency of
production. This latter point is especially important on
longer runs where the consequences of choosing an inappropriate paper for the process can be disastrously expensive,
and it is a good idea to involve the printer in the selection
process where the volume or the value of paper is high. However, once the paper has been selected it is advisable to make

sure that it is specified to all printers who are estimating for the job, to enable valid comparisons to be made.

Depending on the job for which the paper is being specified, paper should be selected on the basis of the type, furnish, finish, end-use requirements, technical properties, and environmental considerations. These factors will largely determine the appearance and feel of the sheet, as well as its printability and runnability.

Type. The main types of commercial papers available can be classified into standard printings, wovens, opaques, high bulk papers, publication papers, newsprint and specials. Within each category there may be a range of types available to suit different needs.

Furnish. Softwoods for papermaking can be either mechanically or chemically pulped, mechanical pulps being cheaper and chemical (or "woodfree") pulps producing papers of a higher quality. Many publication papers aim for a balance of economy and quality by mixing these two types of furnish to produce a part-mechanical paper.

Finish. The most common surface finishes are size, coating and calendering. Different degrees of calendering (polishing with steel rolls) are possible, the most highly-calendered papers being known as supercalendered (or s.c.). Supercalendered papers are particularly suited to gravure printing where very smooth surfaces are essential.

Coatings are applied to give a better printing surface, retaining more of the ink at the surface rather than allowing it to drain in and producing brighter and glossier ink films. They are applied in several different ways, the highest qualities usually being coated at a slower speed on a separate coating machine. Blade coatings and film coatings are applied on-machine for greater economy.

The coating, which is made up of a combination of china clay and chalk, is calendered after coating to produce a smooth surface. High levels of calendering produce a smooth, glossy surface, while matte coateds are made with a lighter calender. Silk mattes are produced in a similar way to the more "toothy" mattes, but with a higher level of calendering to make them smoother. This additional smoothness combats the problem of matte rub, which occurs when minute crystals of calcium carbonate on a matte coated paper have an abrasive action on the ink film of a facing sheet.

The terms "real art" and "matte art" are reserved for the highest quality gloss and matte coated papers, usually with heavy coatings. At the other end of the scale, film coated and lightweight coated (LWC) papers bring good printing performance to the cheaper grades.

Paper Properties   All papers are made to exacting technical specifications that determine their suitability and performance for different types of work. Merchants will normally supply the details of these specifications on request, and they form a useful basis for objective comparison of one paper with another. Some of the more important properties are listed below.

Gloss. Print contrast is enhanced by gloss, and so most images are improved when they are printed on a high-gloss surface. However, many designers feel that the readability of text is impaired by the glare from a gloss surface and prefer a matte coated or uncoated paper. It is possible to mix matte and gloss on the same page by printing a spot varnish (either a matte varnish on a gloss paper or a gloss varnish on a matte paper), and this is often done to increase the contrast of pictures printed on a matte coated paper. Some interesting effects can be achieved by printing text or graphics just as a varnish. Gloss is usually measured according to standards established in the Technical Association of Pulp and Paper Industry (TAPPI) T 480.

Smoothness. Smoothness influences both the feel of a sheet of paper and its ability to print a sharp image. For some jobs, of course, a textured appearance may be preferred, but for fine screens (especially those of 200 lpi and above), or subsequent lamination, smoothness is essential. The usual measure for smoothness is the Bendtsen tester, which indicates smoothness as the rate of air leakage over the paper's surface.

Absorbency. The degree to which a paper absorbs ink will affect the brightness and gloss of printed inks. If the pigments and resins are allowed to sink into the surface the ink will be duller when it dries. More absorbent papers also tend to make printed inks appear slightly warmer in hue than ones with good hold-out. Ink absorbency is usually tested according to TAPPI UM 519, or with the IGT tester.

Smoothness and absorbency are also particularly important for digital printing systems, where it is important to minimize the volume of colorant used and avoid abrasive damage to electrostatic drums.

Whiteness. As well as bleaching the pulp, additives such as calcium carbonate and titanium dioxide are used to improve the whiteness of the paper surface. Whiteness is measured as the spectral reflectance curve of the paper, as described in the ISO whiteness standard.

Brightness. Brightness is a measure of how much light is reflected from a paper surface, and like whiteness is largely controlled by additives to the paper furnish. Brightness is usually tested using either the method described in TAPPI T 452, or using the ISO brightness standard.

Rigidity. This property also contributes to the feel of the paper. Rigidity increases with gsm, but is also affected by the bulk — the less dense the paper, the less rigid it usually is. The usual measure is the Taber stiffness tester, in accordance with TAPPI T 489.

Strength. Several different strength properties may be specified. The tensile strength, for example, will express the resistance of the paper web to breaking during printing, while the burst strength indicates the resistance to forces at right angles to the surface.

Grain direction. Paper fibers line up in the direction of travel during papermaking, and the resulting grain direction is of great importance to printing and folding operations. Paper has more strength across the grain than in the grain direction; it will also tend to expand across the grain when relative humidity increases. Where possible paper should be purchased in sizes that allow the grain direction to run parallel with the main fold in the finished product; in books, brochures and magazines, for example, the grain should run parallel with the spine. Paper is much more likely to crack if the grain runs at right angles to the fold.

Paper Defects   The exacting quality control performed by papermakers makes it unusual for defective paper to be supplied as perfect. In reality, most problems that arise with paper during printing or finishing are caused by choosing a paper whose technical specification makes it unsuitable for the job in hand, or occasionally by production problems that have causes unconnected to the paper chosen (such as excessive ink tack or printing pressures causing fibers to lift from the paper surface).

Defects that do occur on paper range from relatively minor problems that affect the final appearance of the job, such as a caliper or coating weight lower than specified, to potentially more serious problems that can cause major disruptions in production, such as a poorly-bonded surface that leads to coating particles detaching themselves during printing, or inconsistent rolls that can result in frequent web breaks.

Printing defects are more often the result of an incompatibility between the paper and the production process or other materials used in the printed piece. If a coated board cracks during folding, for example, it will normally have happened because the board was not creased before folding and only rarely because there is a defect with the paper surface. Other common causes of incompatibility are inks, varnishes and film lamination.

The paper merchant will always advise on the suitability of a given paper for the printing process, finishing operations, recommended inks, and use of varnishes or lamination. This information is usually given in the technical details of the paper, which can be obtained from the merchant.

Some potential incompatibilities are very hard to predict, and where innovative designs create this kind of risk it is advisable to have full tests done by printing machine proofs and making them up into the finished product, especially if the run is substantial.

Where paper problems do occur during printing or finishing, the merchant should be alerted as soon as possible. The paper supplier will send a technical representative who will determine the nature of the defect and may be able to help the printer to overcome the problem. The printer should not continue with the run once a problem has been identified, as it will be harder to substantiate a claim if production continues (unless printing cannot be delayed and the merchant has agreed to the run continuing). If you are responsible for supplying the paper to the printer you should ensure that evidence is collected in the form of printed and unprinted sheets, and wrappers showing batch and other identification numbers. Always ask the printer to run a few sheets of a similar grade to prove that the paper is indeed the source of the problem.

You can minimize the risk of paper problems by discussing the choice of paper with the printer when the specification for the job is available. You should also endeavor to ensure that there is time allowed in the production schedule for the paper to acclimatize to the conditions of temperature and humidity at the printer or you risk the paper curling at the edges as the fibers absorb moisture and swell — rolls or pallets that have come straight from the mill may need up to three days to reach equilibrium.

Purchasing

Should you leave the purchasing of the paper to the printer or should you contract directly with the merchant or mill yourself? For some buyers there are large savings to be made in going direct, but for others the additional work involved will outweigh any potential gain.

The prime example of a print buyer who should handle the purchase of paper is the publisher with a large volume of printing, using a small range of grades but a number of printers. This publisher may be able to obtain volume discounts unavailable to an individual printer. Printers will legitimately expect to make a handling charge to cover the work involved in unloading and storing the stock, but the size of this charge will be open to negotiation.

At the other extreme, however, many other print buyers with a different profile of work can potentially find direct purchase profitable.

There are several issues to consider if you are thinking of buying paper directly:
- There can be a lot of administrative work involved in handling the purchase and delivery
- You will have a contractual responsibility to the printer for the quality and timeliness of deliveries
- You will need to ensure that overs and wastage quantities are calculated correctly

In practice these issues mean that print buyers need both time and expertise to handle paper purchases successfully, and sufficient volume to make the benefits worthwhile.

Paper merchants and mills have sought to encourage direct sales to a wider range of print buyers in recent years, and recognize that the needs of buyers in this channel are different from the needs of the printer. They will often negotiate payment terms that allow you to take advantage of volume pricing, but issue invoices for part deliveries that are taken over an extended period. They may also agree to handle technical issues that may arise, such as claims made by the printer against the supplier of the paper for defects causing lost production.

If you are considering buying paper yourself it may be worthwhile discussing the options with your printer, who may prefer to reduce their margins rather than have you take the supply out of their hands.

Minimizing the Cost of Paper

Paper can be a major element in the cost of a piece of print (in some cases reaching as much as 50% of the total cost) and it is a good policy to minimize this cost as far as possible. However, reducing costs should not be seen in isolation from the need to maximize the value of a communication, and care should be taken to ensure that this value is not substantially reduced in making a small saving on the cost of paper.

The scope for negotiating price reduction depends mainly on the supply and demand cycle. Price elasticity exists in periods when new capacity has come on-stream and production levels are in excess of demand, and disappears when rising demand absorbs this excess capacity. The only other avenues for reducing the price are to explore the possibility of discounts on larger volumes or on bulk palletized deliveries (eliminating some of the handling costs), or to negotiate with suppliers over the size of the margins they impose to cover handling and profit.

If the possibilities of price reductions have been exhausted, then the buyer can examine the paper specification to see if the same value can be achieved with a different grade or quantity of paper. It may be possible to reduce the total quantity used by:
- Printing fewer copies (for example, by better targeting of the audience)
- Switching to a lighter paper weight (taking care to check on the effects of opacity and handling)
- Using a smaller roll or sheet size by eliminating unnecessary design waste (discuss this option with the printer)

A large amount of print is wasted through being poorly targeted or through over-ordering — although prices for larger quantities may seem attractive, many of the additional copies often end up unused or obsolete. Where the exact quantities that will be needed are not known, it is often better to order for short-term requirements than to print for stock. This approach may mean using just-in-time ordering methods, or considering on-demand digital printing to make short runs cost-effective.

Inks

In the main, ink selection is the domain of the printer who will understand the production processes and the performance requirements of the inks and other consumables used. However, there are occasions where the print buyer may wish to influence the choice of ink in order to maximize the value of the printed piece.

Inks for litho printing are made from a mixture of pigments, resins, oils and small amounts of chemical additives such as drying agents. In other processes the mix is broadly similar, with the substitution of water or other solvents for the oil to make a liquid ink.

Inks are formulated according to the specific performance required, and a very large number of different inks are available to suit the different printing processes and substrates. In litho printing, the formulation may emphasize fast setting (to enable rapid turnaround), high gloss, press stability (to enable the ink to be left on the press for long periods without washing off) or high wax content (to minimize matte rub on matte coated papers). These different formulations are not compatible, so it is not possible, for example, to have both fast setting and high levels of print gloss.

Printers prefer if possible to use the same ink on all types of work, and this usually means a press-stable ink that will reduce the downtime involved in cleaning the press at the end of the day. If a particular job demands a different performance the print buyer will need to request the appropriate type of ink, although there may be an additional charge made for the extra washup.

Other specialized inks that are available include:
- Inks with special optical properties, such as metallic, pearlescent and fluorescent effects
- High-intensity process colors (described below)
- Inks for waterless printing
- Low-odor inks for food packaging

- UV inks that cure instantly on exposure to banks of UV lamps on the press, allowing heavier ink weights to be printed without the risk of setoff
- Microencapsulation inks that release fragrances or dyes when scratched or pressed
- More environmentally-friendly inks (usually with vegetable oils in place of some of the mineral oil content and a lower level of hazardous solvents)

Ink colors for process inks are currently defined in ISO 2846, although the tolerances are not particularly tight and there can be very slight shade variations between inks from different manufacturers. Some ink makers have a high-intensity process set in their range, which gives a larger color gamut than the standard set and can be used as an alternative to high-fidelity (hi-fi) printing in which additional colors are used.

Special colors are usually specified from the Pantone Matching System, which is known worldwide to both designers and printers. The printer may also be able to offer special color libraries from individual ink makers with a range of more vivid colors.

Varnish and Lamination

Gloss and matte varnishes are extensively used to enhance printed communications and protect the surface from damage. Their composition is similar to that of a printing ink but without the pigment, and can be applied in several different ways, including:
- Machine varnishes, which are run on one of the printing units and tend to apply the lowest weight of varnish
- UV varnishes, which are usually printed like machine varnishes but are cured in the same way as UV inks, and give very high gloss levels
- Screen process, which can apply extremely heavy weights of varnish

Varnishes can be applied to the whole sheet or as spot varnishes to specific areas of the page. Overall varnishes are applied more economically on dedicated coating units, which are fitted to the press after the last printing unit.

Varnishing increases the likelihood of cracking on folds. Lamination can be used in its place if this is thought to be a possibility.

Aqueous coatings are a popular alternative to oil-based varnishes. Initially developed for packaging applications, their benefits have led to coating units being installed by many printers outside the packaging sector. They dry extremely fast and thus allow heavier ink weights to be run, and are cheaper than UV varnishes (although they do not achieve quite so high gloss levels).

For packaging, a coating weight of up to 25 grams/meter^2 (gsm) is specified to give barrier protection, while for general commercial printing 5 gsm is sufficient.

Film lamination gives complete barrier protection to the underlying substrate. Lamination can only be applied to the entire sheet (apart from a spot lamination process that can be applied to laser prints and photocopies), and is available in both gloss and matte finishes. If a mix of matte and gloss is required, it is possible to apply spot UV varnish on top of film lamination.

Lamination is quite costly in quantity, but lower setup costs make it cheaper than UV varnish on very short runs (typically 1000 sheets or less).

7   Preparing Artwork

Phil Green

Input

Most artwork for printing is currently prepared in electronic form. Files created by the designer are either sent directly to the printer, who will image the pages onto film ready for platemaking, or to a repro house or bureau which will produce film that can then be sent to the printer.

A typical job will include page make-up files prepared in QuarkXPress or PageMaker, together with transparencies for scanning and laser proofs showing what each page is meant to look like. Pages may incorporate images and graphics supplied as separate TIFF or EPS files. In the case of images, they may be supplied as high-resolution files for incorporating directly into the page, or they may be supplied as low-resolution images for position only, together with the original photographs for the printer to scan and add the resulting high-resolution images to the rest of the page.

In some sectors, such as packaging, powerful proprietary systems known as electronic page composition (EPC) and digital artwork and repro (DAR) are used in preparing work for output on high-end film recorders, or direct imaging onto the printing surface. In others, paper bromides continue to be pasted-up onto artwork boards for photographing on large-format process cameras.

This chapter focuses on the preparation of artwork for PostScript output.

Transparencies and Other Photographic Originals

Despite the rapid growth of digital photography and the widespread use of digital stock libraries, conventional photographic media continue to make up a large proportion of originals supplied for reproduction. These should be carefully protected from possible damage, and marked up to indicate cropping, scaling and any color reproduction preferences.

When selecting photographs for reproduction, consideration should be given to the following points:

- Transparencies usually give better results than prints made from negatives
- When selecting transparencies or prints, or comparing them with proofs, always view them under standard viewing conditions using a 5000K light box or viewing cabinet
- Minor color casts may not be noticeable when transparencies are viewed independently, but viewing several transparencies together may result in a visible difference in color balance — it is a good practice to look at all the pictures that appear on a spread together, and ask for the scanner operator to adjust the color balance if necessary
- As contrast and tonal gradation will be compressed during reproduction, it is essential to choose originals that have well-defined detail throughout the tonal range, especially in the areas of interest of the picture
- Avoid originals with important detail in deep shadow areas, as these are prone to filling-in (especially when the cheaper flatbed scanners are used)

Color retouching after scanning can be very time-consuming and costly. It should be avoided where possible by making sure that good-quality originals are supplied and that any adjustments required are made when the transparency is scanned. Use a 5000K light box to evaluate transparencies and mark up changes to color balance on the transparency mount or sleeve. Note that many adjustments such as overall color cast removal or changes to selected colors can be done at no extra cost, but others, such as alterations to local areas, take much longer and are charged for.

Prints and transparencies are no longer the only source of photographic originals. Digital cameras are now widely used to generate digital images directly without the need for film or scanning (particularly in sectors such as catalog production and news photography). Digital stock libraries provide a source of ready-to-use high-resolution images, often already separated into CMYK.

Some of these image libraries use the PhotoCD file format owing to its ability to store a large number of images on a CD. PhotoCD is also an economical method of scanning and archiving pictures, and retains quality reasonably well, especially when the original media are color negatives.

Electronic Media Page files, graphics and scanned images can be supplied on a variety of electronic media. The medium chosen will depend on the size of the files but also, most importantly, on compatibility with the equipment of the output service.

Floppy disks are used for logos and small EPS graphics, and for jobs consisting of a relatively small number of pages. They cannot be used for scanned images unless a compression utility is used to break the image file into a number of smaller files that can be reassembled later, and this process will add to the time required to process each image.

Removable hard disks (such as SyQuest cartridges and Zip discs) have long been a standard in prepress, and are now available in sizes up to 1 GB. With the proliferation of sizes it cannot be assumed that the output service will be equipped with all types of drive and it is recommended that you check before sending files. Occasionally an output service is unable to read the files on a removable disk due to incompatible software drivers or SCSI chain errors; again, it is advisable to check with the output service before sending files.

Optical discs are also extensively used for high-resolution files, but compatibility problems are even greater than with removable systems, making it imperative to check with the output service.

CD-ROM is extensively used for transfer and archiving of high-resolution files owing to the low cost per megabyte (MB). It also has the advantage that the format is platform-independent, TIFF and EPS files created on any system being readable on any other as long as the ISO 9660 convention has been followed. The low cost of CDs makes it practical to regard them as a once-only medium, avoiding the problems of chasing after costly storage media that have not been returned by the service provider.

Platform The main platforms used in design and prepress are Apple Mac and IBM-compatible PC. Many prepress houses also use high-performance graphics workstations based on the UNIX operating system.

Problems can occur when files are created on one platform and are sent for output on another. Since most corporate organizations are equipped with PCs, while prepress houses have standardized on Macs, it is not unusual for a print purchaser to generate work on a PC and send the files to a Mac-equipped output service. There are solutions to most situations where files need to cross platforms, but unless the output service is used to handling the format you have adopted there can be inconsistencies in output. For example, although most professional graphics programs are now virtually identical on all platforms, some minor formatting commands may be interpreted differently and lead to subtle changes when transferring to another platform. It is best to avoid this situation by finding an output service that uses the same platform as you do, or that has considerable experience in handling work from different platforms.

Applications and File Formats

Aside from the platform issues discussed above, there can be problems if files are submitted in formats not recognized by the output service. The mainstream professional graphics applications such as Adobe PageMaker, Adobe Photoshop, Adobe Illustrator, QuarkXPress, and Macromedia FreeHand are capable of generating files that can be readily imported into other applications and output without difficulty, but with less well-known programs this may not be the case. It is essential to discuss the use of any nonstandard applications or file formats with the printer or output service before sending files.

Graphics should always be saved in EPS format to ensure that they can be imported correctly into page make-up applications. Images can be either EPS or TIFF, depending on the needs of the output device and the structure of the image (for example, which color space has been used).

One reason for using a professional graphics application is that it will be more likely to generate proper EPS files that conform to the document structuring conventions published by Adobe. Applications that take a different route to exporting EPS files can give rise to problems with previews and the rendering of complex details such as overprints, traps and layers.

Fonts

A font is a small program that draws the outline of the characters being printed. The font program needs to be available whenever the font is displayed or printed, and problems regularly arise through the correct font not being available when a page is sent for output; either another font is substituted causing the page to look different (in some cases the new font takes up more space and the text overflows the space allocated), or the job cannot be output at all.

The output device must have the same font available, identical as to manufacturer, name, version, and style. If you have used an unusual font, the output service will have to acquire a copy for their use and may make a charge for this. Note that the practice of sending fonts with the job is frowned on by font developers, and may violate licensing agreements or copyright laws in some countries (such as the U.K. and Germany). However, U.S. copyright law is sketchy at best regarding font protection. Digitized typefaces (and the data used to describe the typefaces) are not protectable by copyright in the U.S.; specific computer programs used to create or store digital typefaces can be copyrighted, but the actual letterform and its accompanying data cannot.

When type is included within graphics such as logos, the font still needs to be available to the output device if it is to be reproduced properly. A technique for avoiding this problem is for the designer to make the fonts used within EPS graphics into path objects (or outlines), so that type is embedded into the file as vector objects and the font is not required when the file is later output. Outlining can be done in most illustration programs. Converting type to outlines in this way changes the appearance of type slightly and can make files much larger (it is recommended only for small amounts of text and is not advisable for smaller type sizes). Outlines cannot be edited as text, so a copy of the file should be made before outlining.

Color

There are several issues to consider in reproducing pages containing color images and graphics.

Composite versus separated files. A color graphic or image normally has three- or four-color components (such as RGB and CMYK). These color components are usually all contained in a single file, in which case the file is known as a composite. For an output device that produces a separate plate from each of the four colors (cyan, magenta, yellow and black), this arrangement is less useful than one in which the components are all in separate files that can be imaged individually. In this type of file format the four files are linked to a low-resolution master or preview file.

Digital printers all require composite files, while many imagesetters require separated files. Although most imagesetter RIPs can now handle composite files, separated files will usually output faster. Most file formats are of the composite variety, with only the EPS DCS format supporting separated colors. DCS 2.0 and above also support files with more than four colors, unlike the TIFF format.

Process *versus* PMS color. The process colors are cyan, magenta, yellow, and black, usually referred to as CMYK. These colors are the printing primaries used in most color printing, and enable a wide range of colors to be reproduced by printing fractional amounts of the four colors.

In many jobs special colors are used. These special colors are arranged in libraries (the most widely used being the Pantone Matching System) and selected from swatches. Most graphics programs allow the selection of both process and PMS colors, and can convert PMS colors to process if required (although different graphics programs often produce different process color values for a given PMS color).

Process and PMS color systems are quite different, and problems can arise from the inappropriate use of each, for example:

- PMS colors are often unwittingly converted to process through selecting the incorrect option in a page make-up program
- If colors are to be printed in CMYK they often look inaccurate and dull if they are selected as PMS and then converted to process (it is better to choose from CMYK tint charts than from PMS color systems if the job is being printed in process color only).

Color management. Achieving a good match to color originals, and to the appearance of the page on screen, is not an automatic process but one which requires careful analysis. Use of appropriate software tools and the calibration of scanner, monitor and output device are all essential to achieve consistent reproduction.

In particular, selecting and approving colors is not simply a matter of looking at something on screen and then expecting it to look exactly the same when printed. There are numerous variables that are virtually impossible to fully account for, and as a result it is always safer to select and approve colors by reference to printed samples, whether color swatches and tint books or color proofs, rather than the screen appearance of a color.

Color management is discussed further in Chapter 8.

Trapping

Trapping is required on any color page where regions of color touch. Because of the difficulty in registering colors with absolute precision on the press (due to slight variations in press register and the expansion of paper during printing) the colors are made to overlap slightly in order to avoid a white hairline appearing between colors. This is a quite straightforward process in manual film assembly: a color is either made to spread slightly into adjacent colors, or the background is made to spread into the foreground color. These two effects are known as spreads and chokes respectively, and are achieved by controlled light diffusion during film contacting.

Figure 7-1.
Prepress workflow from receipt of customer artwork.

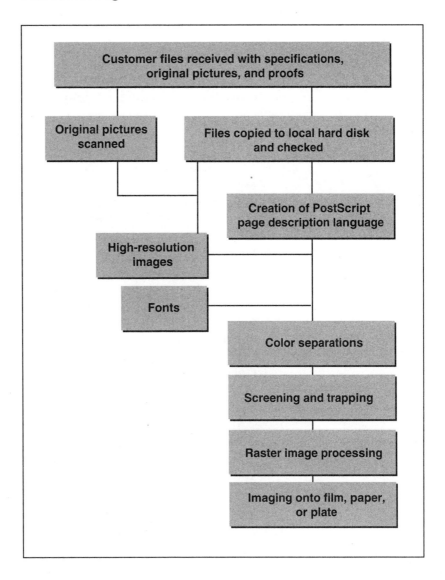

Since the objective of digital page assembly is to output final page films that do not require manual work, trapping needs to be applied at an earlier stage on the digital files. This is an area where errors can be made if the prepress workflow is not managed properly; such cases can result in costly extra work by the output service or in badly trapped pages on the finished job (see Figure 7-1).

Trapping in graphics and page make-up applications is done differently from film-based trapping, as there is no equivalent in the PostScript language to the process of creating an overlap by spreading one color into another. Trapping is thus a technical issue that demands some understanding of trapping concepts, and a knowledge of the printing process and paper being used for the job. Where possible it is preferable to have the trapping done by the output service, but a competent designer should be able to handle it if briefed with information about how wide the traps should be. The printer or output service should be able to advise you on the trap widths.

Trapping can be done at different stages in production:

- Individual graphics that are saved as EPS files can be trapped in the graphics program in which they are created (e.g., Illustrator or Freehand)
- Assembled pages can be trapped in the page make-up program (both QuarkXPress and PageMaker have powerful trap tools, and further functionality can be added in the form of third-party extensions)
- Output services may use a stand-alone trapping application such as Adobe TrapWise or Island Trapper, which provide a greater degree of functionality and automation, and can trap complex color graphics, such as graduations, that graphics and page make-up applications cannot
- Some RIP software is capable of adding traps to the PostScript data stream as it is being processed for output

As a general rule, the later that trapping is applied the better. If you can make use of specialist expertise and software at the output service, you will get more professional results and you may well pay less for them.

Trapping is not always essential. Many sheetfed litho printers regularly achieve sufficient register accuracy that the slight ink spread that causes dot gain is enough to cover up any misregister caused by paper stretch (especially on heavier paper weights or smaller sheet sizes, which are less prone to expansion).

Another way of avoiding the chore of trapping is to use common colors for the background and foreground wherever possible. For example, a dark green that butts up to an orange will need to be trapped, but if the green is made by printing a combination of cyan and yellow with a small amount of magenta, the orange can be made by simply knocking out the cyan from this combination and there is then no need for trapping. This is an example of the robust design approach referred to in Chapter 5.

Imposition

Before plates are made, all the pages on the plate must be arranged in their correct positions, allowing for the folding and binding methods and any special factors like creep allowance.

This process, known as imposition, can be carried out at different stages within the prepress workflow. The most usual procedure is for film to be output in single pages and then positioned manually onto large sheets of clear plastic known as foils. Some printers have the capability to impose pages electronically and output to film on large-format imagesetters. Similar equipment can be used to image plates directly from digital pages without the need to make film.

Since the imposition scheme is determined by the size of the sheet the job is printed on and the way that it will fold, it is usually preferable for the imposition to be carried out by the printer. Large-format imagesetters and platesetters are too costly for publishers (or even most independent output services and repro houses) to contemplate owning.

If you are supplying page film to the printer, consider supplying the pages as a "printer's spread" (two pages arranged as they will appear on the printed sheet before folding, instead of the spread seen by the reader when opening the bound publication — the latter are often referred to by printers as a "reader's spread" to emphasize the difference). This can reduce the cost of imposition, especially on products with a large number of pages. Check before you make this decision, as some printers (especially those who specialize in bookwork) have alternative imposition systems that require single pages.

Be sure to discuss with the printer the requirements for elements like trim marks, bleeds, gutters and so on. The printer may also specify the type of punch register to use when the films are output, if the imagesetter has the ability to punch the film.

Mixing PostScript and non-PostScript Elements

It is often the case that some elements in a printed piece are not supplied in a form that can readily be incorporated into the page for PostScript output. Examples include advertisements that are supplied as film, artist's illustrations prepared on paper or board and files created in a non-PostScript environment such as a high-end EPC system.

To be able to use these elements, one of two things must happen: either they need to be output to film and then assembled manually with the rest of the job; or they must be digitized in some way, either by scanning or by a file conversion process, to bring them into the PostScript environment.

Scanning films can be done with minimal loss of quality on a high-resolution monochrome scanner, which will output the resulting image as a TIFF or EPS file. File conversion requires a "bridge" or "gateway" system that can translate the proprietary high-end format into the PostScript environment.

Before presenting non-PostScript items you should check that the printer has the necessary equipment to handle them.

Optimizing Output

To achieve efficient output of PostScript files, it is essential to avoid creating unnecessary work at the RIP stage. When a PostScript file is output (regardless of whether it is sent to an imagesetter, digital printer or low-resolution page printer), most of the work done by the RIP consists of processing the vector commands in the page file that recreates type and graphics and the raster data that define scanned images.

The amount of data in a scanned image, and thus the amount of processing, is fixed by the size, resolution and color depth of the image, and there is little room to alter this. However, the amount of vector processing can vary hugely according to the way that the page and any EPS graphics were constructed. The more complex the shapes used in defining graphics, the longer they will take to output. Some of this complexity may not be essential, being a consequence of the methods employed in creating the graphics rather than a necessary element of the design. Designers should take care to use appropriate techniques in preparing graphics and cut-out images, and placing them on the page. Particular points to note are:

- Scaling and cropping of images should be done in an image editing program wherever possible, not in a page make-up application
- Rotating or scaling an EPS graphic should ideally be done in the graphic application in which it was created, before it is imported into the page make-up application

Minimize the number of graduations and blends on a page, unless they are converted from a vector graphic to a raster (pixel-based) file format. Use the EPS rasterizer in Photoshop, or in the illustration program used to create the graphic, to do this conversion.

Draw clipping paths for image cut-outs that are to be exported to a page make-up application with a path tool, rather than a selection tool such as a magic wand. Drawing the clipping path makes it much smoother and less complex than selecting it.

Construct all paths as simply as possible; the designer should split very long or complex paths and the number of points used to define a path should be minimized by setting a curve flatness of 8 pixels or more. (Splitting paths and setting curve flatness are simple menu options in professional graphics applications.)

Sending a document for output that disregards these points will add considerably to output time and risks encountering resource limits that cause the output to fail altogether.

Output Checklist   Carry out the following checks before files are sent for output:

- Do a Save As in your page make-up application. Any changes that you make during the creation of a page are usually just added to the end of the file. The Save As command rebuilds the file and removes any redundant data.
- Remove any fonts that are not needed in the final version of your document. Confirm with the output service that they have copies of the fonts that you are using.
- Delete any pages that are not being printed.
- Check the requirements of the output service for disk and file formats.
- Check that trapping has been done on placed EPS files, or that you have requested the output service to trap them for you.

- Check the page set-up and scaling settings. These are saved with the document and will be used by the output service unless you have specified otherwise.
- Check all the links to placed images and graphics, updating as necessary.
- Check that all required images and graphics are included in the files being sent for output.

Output Problems   Ideally, the files should be supplied in a form that can be output fast and efficiently without errors. In reality, the handover between the purchaser and the printer is often beset by problems. Production is delayed and extra costs are incurred due to unnecessarily extended output times and avoidable errors.

Output errors have three origins. Most common are design-level errors (such as incorrect trap settings or color specification); next come output-level errors (mistakes made by the output service personnel); finally there are application-level errors (unexpected errors that arise from the design of user applications or the output device interpreter).

Virtually all these errors are avoidable. If designers follow guidelines for preparing electronic files, the output service follows the correct procedures for file output, and the applications used conform to PostScript language rules, then very few errors should occur.

Preflight Checks   Despite carefully assembling a document, it is still possible to see it cause problems when it is output; it might fail during output, or create some snag that ties up the imagesetter for an unreasonable amount of time; or alternatively an unexpected error may be introduced into the document.

One way of testing that a file will output correctly is to simulate the output process. This is sometimes known as "preflighting."

Of course, this is done to some extent when you make a proof on a PostScript laser printer. However, it is possible for some problems to fail to show up at this stage, either because the laser printer has a much lower resolution than an imagesetter or because the PostScript RIP treats PostScript language commands in a slightly different way.

An alternative to sending the page files created by the page make-up application is to send them as Acrobat files. From version 3.0, released in September 1996, Acrobat PDF files are able to incorporate all the information that would be found in the PostScript code created by a page make-up application (including trapping, color management and OPI information). Because a PDF file is structured differently from a PostScript file (it is a database of everything on a page, rather than a program to paint the objects on an output device) it is much more robust and less prone to errors during output.

This approach also means that the contents of the page can be effectively previewed on screen, as the Acrobat file is a complete record of the page as it will output. Adobe has signalled their intention to put Acrobat at the heart of future workflow architectures, such as the Supra architecture for multi-processor RIPs and distributed printing.

Sending Files Electronically

In many cases files are now sent by communications link rather than physical media, the advantage being faster transfer with the elimination of the costs of courier services and media. Most printers and output services can accept files electronically, either by direct modem connection or by receiving the files from a third-party Internet service provider.

Modems may be used for small graphics and page files, but are impractical for the larger file sizes used by scanned images. ISDN is becoming more widespread, although it offers only medium bandwidth, and is relatively expensive to install and use. Fiber-optic links, if available, offer a faster and more economical means of sending files.

Since hard copy proofs will normally still be needed, you should fax laser prints directly to the supplier together with your output specification. It is recommended that you compress files before sending (preferably as a self-extracting archive) using a standard compression utility.

Software utilities to assist in the process of assembling and transferring jobs to your service provider are now available. ISDN software packages often have useful functions such as soft proofing built in, and applications such as Adobe Virtual Network are designed to enable remote delivery of files which are routed automatically to job queues at the output service. Virtual Network, which works with most high-speed communications links including ISDN, also returns files in Acrobat format to the customer for approval.

Bringing Prepress In-House

The purchaser of printed products is increasingly taking on aspects of production formerly the province of the printer or repro house, and this trend is certain to continue. It is possible to foresee a situation where the normal mode of production is for the purchaser to carry out all prepress functions, leaving only the ink-on-paper stage to be handled by the printer — and that only on production volumes too great to be handled by in-house digital printing equipment.

This approach is driven by the cost and control benefits that can be achieved, and is increasingly supported by new desktop prepress technologies. It leads to a significant reduction in prepress costs, and faster turnaround of work in progress. As the job remains in the control of the purchaser up until the point when it goes on press, late alterations can be made without cost or schedule penalties.

However, the further in-house production reaches into downstream production operations, the more technically complex the issues that will arise and have to be dealt with. For a job to be produced efficiently it is essential that each stage in production has been carried out correctly, and that there is an assurance that the efficiency of later stages of production will not be adversely affected. As purchasers move further into the production arena they take on increasing responsibility for prepress decisions, and for directly managing the work of those responsible for design and prepress.

Prepress Specification

If you are supplying films to the printer (whether they have been output by the designer, a repro house, or another printer) it is vital that the output service is made aware of the requirements of the printing process and the substrate that you are using. Ideally, the two suppliers will communicate these details directly, but if not, you may need to convey the information to the output service before the films are output. This information should form part of a prepress specification, which should cover the following points:

- Job information:
  - Final page size
  - File name of document
  - File format and compression software used
  - Page make-up application used
  - Scale for output (if not 100%)
  - List of all files used in the document
  - List of all fonts used in the document

- Proofs required
- Special colors used
- Special services requested (including trapping, color correction and image retouching)
- A list of all materials supplied, including laser prints and photographic originals
- Press information:
  - Dot gain
  - Screen frequency
  - Screening technology
  - Positive or negative film
  - Emulsion up or down

The printer should be consulted about the press information section. If you do not know who the printer will be when you are ready to have the job output, accept the output service's recommendations or use the relevant industry standard (see Chapter 8). For sheetfed litho on coated paper a screen frequency of 150 lines/in. (60 lines/cm) using a conventional screen and 18% midtone dot gain, and negative emulsion-down film, will usually be acceptable.

8 Prepress Production

Tony Johnson

The technology associated with prepress production has caused radical structural changes to the industry in recent years, although the origins of this can be traced back to the mid-to-late 1970s when digital computing was introduced into prepress. At that time the minicomputers and other custom-made components used for these tasks made the systems very expensive.

However, during the 1980s the advent of new detector technologies (in particular, CCD arrays) and more powerful and cheaper electronics enabled a radical cost reduction of digital scanners, albeit with lower quality, and the development of personal computers in both the IBM and Macintosh formats. This led to the production of user-friendly mass-market software with many of the features of the prepress software available to the professional repro producer, but at a low cost and providing relatively low quality, frequently being run on platforms with very limited speed, and output on plain-paper printers for subsequent copying.

To differentiate work produced on such systems from the more complex and higher quality work produced on the faster minicomputer-based systems, the terms DTP (desktop publishing) and CEPS (color electronic pagination systems) were often used to differentiate them.

Since then the speed of the personal computer has been enhanced, and the features available in the software packages have become similar to those available in the proprietary systems. Today, a PC or Mac provided with sufficient memory for the efficient handling of images can approach the performance of the fastest of the proprietary systems, while the workstations (such as the Sun or Silicon Graphics systems) have come even closer. They all have the added advantage of being far more open than the proprietary systems, thereby enabling other software packages to be run if required, and enable images and pages to be moved between systems with far greater ease.

Because of this the industry has undergone a radical change, and many designers and publishers are producing their own digital artwork for reproduction (DAR), and providing the final pages to the trade house or printer for imagesetting onto film or plate. Any differentiation between DTP and CEPS has all but disappeared and the time has really come to drop the terms.

Various other developments at the time of writing, which are having an impact on the production of images for printing, include digital photography, PhotoCD and FM screening. In fact, as will be discussed in the technology sections which follow this introduction, none of them really alter the basic imaging issues. The quality of images obtained during reproduction still depends upon well understood rules, and the "new" technologies simply provide different ways of achieving these. However, they do offer a new convenience which a print buyer may be able to use. This issue will be returned to later.

Image Capture

Many of the images seen today are wholly computer-designed, but by far the majority are natural scenes or paintings which need to be reproduced in print. For the purposes of print production, most natural scenes originate on photographic material, but there is an increasing trend towards the use of digital cameras which enable the scene to be recorded directly as digital data with no photographic intermediate. As the quality of these devices improves, the number of images originating in this form will increase significantly.

However, for the purposes of the discussion in this section, which focuses on the technology of image capture, there is no need to differentiate them from scanners which digitize hard copy. The charge-coupled device (CCD) technology is similar, and the requirements for high-quality imaging are more or less identical. In fact, many of the so-called digital cameras in current use are really scanners. They employ a linear CCD array (in which thousands of individual detectors, each approximately 10–15 microns wide, are formed in a single line on a silicon "chip"). This is positioned in the image plane of a camera, and then scans across the image plane just as a scanner would. Inevitably they take several minutes to achieve this, which means that they are only useful for capturing scenes which are static for long periods.

True digital cameras with acceptable quality are now emerging. In these, the CCD elements form a two-dimensional array containing millions of detector sites. This means that the whole image can be captured in a fraction of a second, just as for photographic film. The reason for the relatively slow evolution of this technology is the problem in manufacturing CCD arrays with sufficient sites that maintain the uniform properties needed for high-quality imaging. This is now being overcome, but inevitably such devices are still rather expensive. Thus, high-quality digital cameras using this technology will not be cheap until the manufacturing process for the CCD arrays improves. This development is, however, almost inevitable.

The scanner or camera has to separate a color image into its red, green and blue components. This means that the device has to have three detectors (or detector arrays), each with the appropriate colored filter in front of it, or alternatively to capture the image three times, each time with the appropriate filter in front of the detector.

Another significant development in CCD technology which is enabling the cost of such scanners to fall, or performance to improve, is the introduction of these filters on to the detector array itself. This is absolutely essential for the true digital camera which can capture moving images. Obviously, it means that to maintain resolution three times as many elements are required for color as for monochrome.

In order to obtain high-quality reproductions, the image capture device must provide a good specification for five main features. Any print buyer who is responsible for purchasing prepress should be aware of the impact of these features on image quality before having images scanned, and should keep a set of test images which will enable such evaluation. Historically the highest quality has always been obtained from scanners that use photomultiplier (PM) technology for sensing the light reflected or transmitted by the image when it is scanned by a beam of light incident on a rotating drum.

There is no fundamental reason why those scanners using CCD technology should provide lower quality. However, scanner design is more critical to optimize the features of importance, and so the quality obtained from CCD scanners is always likely to be marginally lower for reasons to be described below. But, as this difference decreases it is increasingly offset by the ease of use of CCD scanners in relation to copy loading on a flat bed, and for this reason the sales of PM scanners will continue to diminish.

Resolution. A high resolution not only provides reproduction of fine detail but also ensures that images are sharp and high contrast. To understand this, consider the scanning of a sharp edge which is black on one side of the edge and white on the other. The digital signal obtained is a product of the light reflected or transmitted by the sample, as seen by the detector. If the area imaged by an individual detector is large and the resolution low the resultant digital data will make the sharp edge look like a gray ramp since the probability is that the signal obtained at the edge will contain some white and some black. The low resolution means that the gray edge will be quite wide. So, to obtain a digital signal which reproduces the sharp edge reasonably accurately, the area imaged by the detector must be small and the resolution high.

Experience tells us that an image that reproduces sharp edges accurately not only provides more detail but also produces a perceptual phenomenon in which it looks more contrasting. This is why edges of scanned images are artificially enhanced by a process often known as USM (unsharp masking). To a limited degree this can overcome the effect of low resolution; however, there is a limit to this.

Clearly, a high scan rate is required for a high resolution, but does not guarantee it unless the area imaged by the sensor is related to the scan rate. Scanning with a high resolution, but where a large area of the image is imaged for each pixel, provides a resultant edge which is little better than the scan made with the low resolution (although the potential for image processing is higher). In such situations we talk of a high addressability. On a PM scanner, minimizing this effect means choosing the correct aperture. On a CCD scanner, resolution can be limited in this way when any movement of the sensor array is employed, such as in the direction of scan on linear array scanners, or where any "dithering" of the CCD is used. (This is a procedure whereby the CCD is moved by a few microns a number of times during each scan position. The resultant data provides the additional addressability.)

Artifacts of the array, such as charge spilling into adjacent sensor sites, or not fully discharging between scan lines, or

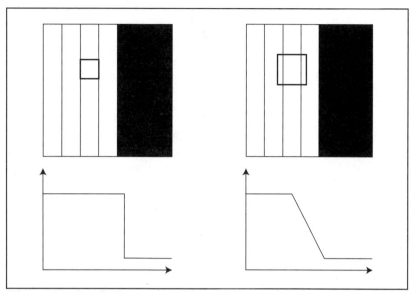

Figure 8-1. Resolution versus addressability. In the left diagram the scanning aperture is exactly the same size as the scanning pitch and the image edge is exactly aligned to the scan. Assuming that there are no electronic bandwidth constraints, the output signal obtained is a perfect "step" as shown in the lower left. However, for the right diagram, the aperture is twice the size of the scanning pitch. The output obtained with this has a "soft" edge as shown in the lower right diagram. Both scanners have the same addressability but the left one has twice the resolution of the right in its ability to clearly reproduce fine lines. Because the image will rarely align with the scanning pitch the resolution is generally half that of the scanning pitch for the ideal left case and a quarter for the more typical right case. Note that many manufacturers quote resolution when they really mean addressability.

too low a bandwidth in the electronics on either type of scanner, can cause similar effects to those obtained by too low a resolution or high addressability (namely a lack of sharpness and detail) but these properties are continually being improved by the manufacturers of the CCD chips.

In order to calculate the scanning rate required for reasonable quality reproduction, a rough rule of thumb is that for the size of the image to be output a scanning rate of approximately 300 dpi (12 dots/mm) is needed. This provides 300 pixels/in. (12 pixels/mm) if no interpolation of the scanned data is used, and this is the most desirable situation.

Interpolation can be used quite effectively to obtain a reasonable number of pixels per inch from a lower scan rate but the effects are to increase addressability rather than resolution (although the relationship is not quite so simple). In general it is desirable to scan the image at the highest rate possible but the file size grows rapidly since it is proportional to the square of the scanning rate. A scan rate of 300 dpi (12 dots/mm) can be considered to be an adequate compromise. This basic scan rate is then multiplied by the enlargement factor to obtain the actual scanning rate for that image.

Of course, if the final size of the image is unknown at the time of scanning, the image should be scanned at the rate required for the maximum enlargement likely, and interpolated downward when the final size is known. Using a reasonable interpolation algorithm, the only detrimental effect of this is that the file size may be large. For higher quality, a basic scanning rate (before multiplying by the enlargement factor) of approximately 400 dpi (16 dots/mm) may be desirable, while approximately 150 dpi (8 dots/mm) may be adequate for less critical applications.

On many scanners, the scanning rate is fixed and the image has to be produced by mathematical interpolation of the scanned data. The quality of the interpolation algorithm used is very important. As already stated, a poor one can introduce similar effects to scanning at a high addressability; the image loses its detail, sharpness and contrast.

Thus, the print buyer should ensure that any images scanned produce the file size required for output, based on the selected scanning rate, and ensure that the scanner produces an acceptable resolution and avoids aliasing (jagged edges on sharp detail) by using suitable test images and employing a good color separation and unsharp masking package and output device.

A set of transparencies with properties similar to the various digital test images standardized in ISO/DIS 12640 and provided on CD would be very useful for this purpose. Although Kodak and Fuji no longer sell sets of prints and transparencies for such evaluation, a very good set for this purpose can be obtained from the Graphic Arts Technical Foundation in Pittsburgh (see Appendix 1 for the address). The digital images on the ISO CD offer an excellent guide to the type of features on the transparency that should be selected. The only other requirements are that the test images should be sharp and fine grain, although it is useful to also have a coarse grain and less sharp image included to see how the scanner and image processing deals with them.

Data resolution. All digital scanners are characterized by the number of bits of digital data that they produce (quantize). In principle, this defines the number of gray levels that can be differentiated since the number of separate values that can be specified is the value 2 raised to the power of the number of bits. Thus 8 bits of data provides 2^8 separate values (i.e., 256), each of which could be a separate level of gray. However, this figure alone is not very meaningful. Even if we assume that every level of quantified data really does represent a different gray level (which is not always the case) we also need to know the domain in which the data is quantified. Eight bits of reflectance or transmittance data obtained by simply measuring the proportion of incident light reflected or transmitted by the scanner is not enough. It will give rise to contouring effects in the darker part of the images (see Figure 8-2). With such data, 14 to 16 bits (16,384 to 65,536 quantization levels) is required to produce high-quality results while 12 (4,096 levels) is somewhat marginal. However, if some analog electronics are employed to introduce a mathematical transformation to the analog data prior to quantization, which ensures that the data is better "spaced" perceptually, such as producing the cube root or log of the reflectance/transmittance data, 8 bits is just about adequate, though 9 or 10 would be better. The same may be achieved by quantizing to, say, 14 bits at the scanner and then doing the mathematical transformation to cube-root or log digitally, prior to storing as 8 bits.

Figure 8-2.
Left The image shows the effect of inadequate precision. Note the obvious contours and bands.

Right The image is quantized with adequate precision.

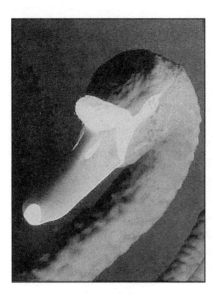 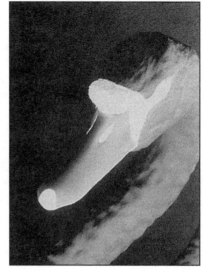

Noise. When scanning a uniform region of color many scanners exhibit a level of "graininess" that generally comes from noise in the detector and associated electronics. This can be particularly obvious in the darker tones. The problem is often enhanced by the image processing software, such as the unsharp masking algorithms used to enhance the sharpness of the image. It can be singularly intrusive on certain images, although it sometimes hides the effects of limited data resolution. Other common sources of unevenness which may be visible are streaks coming from inadequate correction of varying sensor sensitivity in a CCD linear array, or uneven illumination and dust or scratch marks coming from an inadequate copy mounting procedure.

Dynamic range. The range of gray levels, from light to dark, which a scanner can record is very variable. One limiting factor is the number of bits that the scanner can resolve, but the most significant limiting factor is flare in the optical system. For PM scanners, this is relatively easy to overcome because of the simplicity of the optical system in which only a single spot is imaged at a time. For CCD scanners or cameras, the problem is more difficult because multiple spots are being imaged simultaneously. Only small amounts of flare need to arise to significantly reduce the darkest tones that can be resolved, and such flare can be induced by scattering the light from other parts of the image being scanned at the same time. Thus, despite the fact that CCD devices have a dynamic range that approaches that of photomultipliers, many scanners using the same technology have significantly poorer dynamic range.

Color discrimination. The choice of separation filters in the scanner can affect its ability to discriminate color. There are two conflicting requirements, particularly when considered in conjunction with the issues of noise and data resolution. The result is generally some sort of compromise. On one hand the filters should be broad band to simulate those of the eye. This ensures that metameric colors (those which look the same but contain different pigments or dyes, thereby producing different reflectance or transmittance throughout the visible spectrum) are scanned the same.

At the same time, to minimize noise from cross-talk (whereby information from one channel is passed into another), and maximize the signal differentiation between the lightest and darkest channels in each pixel, the filters should be narrow band. In practice many scanners, because they are only scanning photographic materials with a limited range of pigments, tend to the latter, whereas digital cameras, which may encounter any pigment, tend to the former. This means that the ability of different devices to obtain good color discrimination can vary and should be checked by using suitable test images.

Image Transfer and Raster Image Processing

After images have been scanned, they are normally combined with others and merged with text and computer generated elements such as vignettes, borders and tints to form a page. Following this, they are loaded onto some transportable media, or transmitted over a network, to the site where they are rendered onto film, proof or plate—often the printing site itself. This step usually requires the pages to be processed in some way, either to generate raster files (in which the pixels are defined as consecutive lines of data required by the line recording mechanism of the output device) or convert the image in some specific way.

Image media and file formats. Increasingly CD will be the medium of choice for the transfer of images and pages, but removable cartridge, shuttle, and erasable optical discs will continue to have their roles. The print buyer must ensure that the media specified is compatible with everybody in the production chain. However, ensuring the correct media is only part of the story. In order that a file may be read by another user, it is important that the file format is intelligible to the receiving system. To this end *defacto* standards have arisen which are now evolving into *dejure* standards. For images of all varieties, but particularly color "contone" images (whereby the image is defined in its unscreened, gray-level form), TIFF has almost become the *defacto* standard. It obtains its openness by defining, uniquely, a variety of tags that can take on certain defined values. These define a whole series of parameters, such as color, resolution, size, data range and orientation, that are needed to interpret the image data. ISO has now standardized an extension of this as TIFF/IT for graphic arts applications. For separated images, included as part of a page, EPS files are the more common format. This will be discussed later.

Where pages being received require no correction, PostScript has proved to be a popular basis for page definition and hence as a transfer standard. However, PostScript was primarily developed for the purposes of processing mixed raster-vector pages into raster form prior to, or at the time of, output. So, before discussing its use as a file format for data exchange, we need to consider its role as a raster image processor.

Raster image processing. This process, usually known as "ripping," converts pages into raster form at the resolution required for output, and the software includes such features as screening, color separation, chokes and spreads (also known as trapping), and interpolation. The quality of these functions are fundamental in defining the quality of the final printed page. PostScript is by far the most popular and comprehensive raster image processing software available. It is a programming language that defines various facets of graphical objects and text and their position in a page. A page layout is converted by the application into a series of Post-Script commands which accompany the images contained in the page. It is then interpreted by a software package at the receiving site, normally at the same time as the image is output, when the resolution of the device is known.

Unfortunately, the various applications tend to handle the creation of the code in different ways and interpreters may render a set of commands differently than others. Although Adobe tries to prevent this by authorizing interpreters, it is not possible to remove this variability completely, particularly for complex pages. Thus, a page may not render exactly as intended by the producer. It may even fail to output at all. This can be very frustrating, particularly since it is often tedious to work around this problem. It seems likely that Adobe's PDF (portable document format used in its Acrobat software and heavily based on PostScript) will become increasingly popular as it is incorporated into other software packages and some of the problems are removed.

Returning to the use of PostScript as a file format, it may now be clearer why it can serve such a dual purpose. The two requirements are really very similar. However, a fully editable version is really needed. Of course, PostScript could be editable if read and interpreted by a suitable application package but for the reasons given above this is not really recommended, unless it is read by the application package that created it. Files are normally saved as EPS (encapsulated PostScript) files, which enables another application to use them in another document but without interpreting them. A good standard for page formats that permits editability is still badly needed.

Other file format issues. Apart from file format and media, a number of other issues need to be resolved by a user when passing a file from one place to another. The main ones that need to be specified by the print buyer are the color "space" the file should be saved in, whether the data should be compressed, and the availability of the fonts in the page.

The color "space" chosen really depends on where in the process the exchange is occurring. However, any file transfer that occurs after contract proofing should be in separated format, normally CMYK. For control purposes, it is desirable to include a target containing specified dot percent values in each color along with the file. Dot values of 5%, 25%, 50%, 75%, 95% and 100% are recommended. By including the data with the file, and insisting on it being output with the page, all parties can ensure that the page has been correctly rendered. This is easy on film where the target can be exposed in an area where it can be cut off, but is not so easy in a direct-to-plate environment (although the plate areas outside the paper area may be used). This target should not be confused with the print control bar, which typically only contains two (50% and 100%), or at most four (25%, 50%, 75% and 100%), of the above values. The additional values are needed to ensure no artifacts are introduced in the important highlight and shadow ends by poor calibration during plate or film production, and are akin to those used in the platemaking control elements.

For gray-level images, the choice of whether or not to use data compression is a complex one, whereas for binary images it is far easier. The decision depends upon two issues: will the compression system cause any change to the file, and does the calculation time make it worthwhile for the amount of compression obtained? The most popular lossless systems (run length and LZW encoding) are very effective on binary files, but less so on grayscale images. Raster binary files are usually large and will always benefit from lossless compression.

The compression obtained with a lossless system is invariably small unless the image contains a lot of uniform areas of color, and for "busy" images the file may even expand. This unpredictability makes lossy systems (in which some information is removed) desirable for efficient compression of a grayscale file. The most important is based on a mathematical process known as a discrete cosine transform (DCT), and this is the basis of an ISO standard known as JPEG. An average compression ratio of 8:1 is acceptable for a range of images (the actual value is image-specific), although some artifacts are visible on the separations but not so visible on the proofs. However, it must be said that to the sharp-eyed observer, artifacts may even be visible on the proof at this level, and so care is needed in using it.

The choice of type fonts in a page can cause serious difficulties because of licensing issues. Since copyright laws in the U.S. are so unclear regarding fonts and digitized typefaces, licensing agreements usually include specific statements regarding third-party use of font information. Some companies allow fonts to be transferred providing that the recipient of the information has a license to use the software containing the font. However, the range of fonts available is so large that it is impractical to expect any receiver to have a license to use any font incorporated in a design. What is really required is a clearly-stated legal situation that allows a font to be sublicensed by the owner of the license, solely for the duration of the job being done, and provided to the printer or trade house with the job for output, on condition that it be removed from the RIP immediately once the job is completed. Embedding the job in a file in such a way that it is difficult to separate would help.

Failing this, the buyer has three choices. Either find a service provider who definitely has all the fonts required, or accept substitution of other fonts (which may well cause difficulty in that the different fonts do not take up the same space in the page) or rip the page prior to sending it to the service provider (which is inefficient and makes for large files).

Image Output

At the time the image is output it will normally be ripped as described above. At the same time a number of other possible operations may be undertaken. The most important of these is the selection of the halftone screen (if not specified in the file), color transformation (if not already separated), calibration (both of the output device itself, often known as linearization compensation for dot gain), and imposition (including provision of print color bars).

These parameters are normally defined at the time of output by the provider of the output service. However, it is important that the print buyer specifies precisely what is required in order to achieve the desired result. If default settings are used, a disappointing result is quite likely unless the print buyer has ensured that such settings suit the reproduction process (scanner and print process) to be used.

Halftone screening. Regular screens should be chosen to be the finest possible ruling consistent with the printing process and paper being printed on. Frequency-modulated screens (also known as stochastic screens) should have the finest element size consistent with satisfactory process control. Each halftone dot is constructed from smaller exposed spots, the number of which is determined by the resolution of the exposing device. (The spots exposed by the output device are often referred to as "device pixels.") However, it is important for other reasons than screening that the resolution is not too low. In particular the reconstruction of line work, borders and text will lead to aliasing and the inevitable jagged edges. To avoid this, a rough rule of thumb is that the resolution of the

Figure 8-3.
An individual halftone dot is built from the array of device pixels defined by the output device address grid.

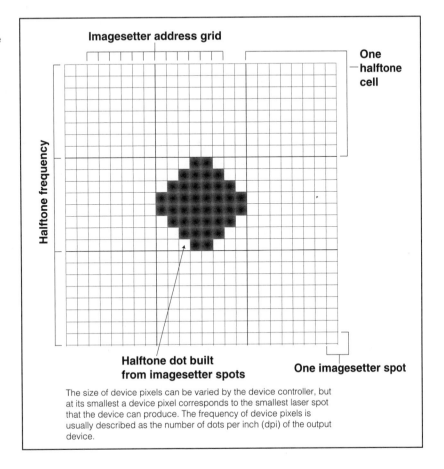

Imagesetter address grid

One halftone cell

Halftone frequency

Halftone dot built from imagesetter spots

One imagesetter spot

The size of device pixels can be varied by the device controller, but at its smallest a device pixel corresponds to the smallest laser spot that the device can produce. The frequency of device pixels is usually described as the number of dots per inch (dpi) of the output device.

recording device should be approximately 2000 dpi (at least 80 dots/mm) and is more typically 2400 dpi (100 dots/mm). This resolution means that something like 6 to 10 lines of dotsare recorded per pixel of image data, and this can be used to advantage in halftone dot generation in minimizing the noise and/or permitting fairly high screen frequencies to be reproduced. To a large extent, this text and line work requirement nullifies the often-claimed advantage of FM screens enabling lower resolution recording; in general FM screen elements are produced from more than one exposing spot!

These high resolutions explain why there is no direct correlation between the screen frequency and the input scanner resolution. The image reconstruction is determined by the recorder resolution, and hence, even for a low screen frequency, better results will always be obtained by increasing the scanner resolution, at the expense of file size. However, many people recommend a rough rule of thumb to be that the scanner resolution should be twice the screen frequency (multiplied by the enlargement). On the basis of the 300-dpi (12 dots/mm) scan rate described earlier, this formula provides a 150-lpi (60 lines/cm) screen, which can be taken as fairly typical.

Color transformation. If the file is not in the color space required for the output device, a color transformation will be required. In general such a file will be encoded in the RGB space defined by the scanner, but increasingly it will be accompanied by a tag that defines how it is related to the internationally accepted CIE system of color measurement. This information can be used to set up a color transformation that notionally converts the RGB data into the equivalent CIE data and from that into the output device drive signals required to achieve this color. Because of issues to do with measurement limitations, the effect of viewing conditions on different media causing differences of appearance on samples having the same CIE values and the differences in color gamut between the different media, the transformation is not as simple as suggested above. The color management system used to calculate the color transformation has to be capable of compensating for these effects in achieving high quality, and it is this that differentiates a good color management system from the rest.

Calibration. It has to be ensured at the time of output that the device is properly calibrated for the process it is being used for. By calibration we mean that the device is brought to some state that is consistent from day to day. This calibration is often used to combine two requirements: linearization of the film (or plate) recorder/media combination, and correction for the output device characteristics. The latter is no more than the color transformation described in the previous section, but if data has already been converted for the output device characteristics, any further transformation required at output is usually reduced to a simple single dimensional correction in each color channel (C, M, Y, or K) because of the similarity in ink color across many of the different processes. It can then be combined with the linearization process, which ensures that the dot percent values specified in the file, or by the color transformation, are correctly rendered on the film or plate.

Should You Buy or Produce Your Own Prepress?

Producing one's own prepress is, in principle, quite simple. However, the practice is not quite so easy. Establishing whether it is best to buy or produce one's own color prepress means no more than thinking through a number of seemingly obvious factors in a logical way. The result of this process should enable you to decide the best route forward. The suggestions and discussion below are but one approach; the specifics depend upon your own procedures. Nevertheless, it may help you to develop you own strategy.

The major issues that the user must consider are:
- Quality
- Cost
- Convenience
- Quantity of images or pages to be produced
- Skill level
- Openness of the system

As with most things in life you get what you pay for. High quality invariably means high-cost equipment, although a lot of the cost may also be dedicated to high productivity. Thus producing the highest quality color reproductions may well require the outlay of high capital expenditure. However, it is possible to get reasonable quality at lower cost by forgoing the productivity, and so it should not be assumed that all cheap equipment means low quality. Thus, the decision must start by considering the quality and number of images, or pages, per day that you require.

Once this is known, it is sensible to find out the cost of doing this amount of work from a number of full-service providers. Take some example pages and obtain quotations for this work, given the throughput you require. Ensure that any special requirements are understood, and in fact whether these are easily grasped may provide a measure of the quality of the provider. Also obtain samples of their work, using test procedures such as those outlined above. It is also useful to get them to break down their quotes so that you can establish whether it is sensible for you to produce some of the work, and for them to produce the rest. For example, they may do scanning and output to film or plate while you do page assembly.

This will provide your yardstick. Now take the same test images and pages, and talk to equipment vendors. Establish the capital and running costs of the equipment and add to it the maintenance and overhead costs (labor, space, heat, light and power) associated with it. From this it is easy to establish whether producing your own prepress is cost-effective, or at least whether any additional cost is offset by the convenience.

You should also think about your own skill levels. If you have struggled with any of the concepts discussed in this chapter, be wary. Many people tell you how easy it is to buy a variety of products and simply plug them together. However, experience shows that it is never quite so simple. When the problems arise, be sure you have the skills to determine which part of the process is causing the problem. Think about how you can separate the process into its component parts, by using suitable test images and procedures, and interpret the results. If you cannot do this, be sure you have the support of a systems integrator or vendor who can do it for you.

If, having got this far, you still want to proceed with your own production, then expand your discussions with equipment vendors. Ensure you get test images, which provide insight into the issues discussed under image capture, produced on a number of input devices and in a number of formats. Take those images to the output device vendors, and get them output together with standard test images such as the ISO images referred to earlier. Get everything printed by your selected printing process. By comparing all of these factors, you can establish the best scanner or camera for your needs as well as the best output device.

Think about various production techniques as you grapple with all of the above. Consider whether a digital camera or a scanner meets your needs; is your work suited to a digital camera environment, such as catalog production, or is it such that you are going to continue to use photographic media to some degree? When considering purchasing prepress, decide whether you can use any of the mass production scanning services such as PhotoCD. This offers the potential of cheapness and reasonable quality if the professional PhotoCD format is employed. However, if all you need is the convenience of images on CD, do you actually want the PhotoCD format? Does it bring you any real benefit in communicating with others? If not, a more flexible format (such as TIFF) may be preferable. Consider how you will proof images or pages prior to output. If you are not using a proofing process based on film, how confident can you be that it will be a satisfactory predictor of the printed result? Use test images to evaluate this. Think about what your output requirements are (in terms of film, plate, etc.) and how you will achieve this. What sort of halftone screening do you require and how well can your printer handle it? Fine screens and FM screens offer certain quality advantages, but does your printer employ the process control needed to make them work? Will you use an output service, and if so, what file formats do you need?

The list of such questions can go on for many pages, and we would still not have them all. You need to consider your own process and formulate the appropriate questions for yourself. If you don't know the answers, ask the vendors and their competitors, or go to an independent consultant. Remember, however, only you know your own requirements and it is impossible to overstress the importance of thinking through carefully, and in as quantifiable a way as possible, what you require, before talking to any service providers and equipment vendors.

Preparation for Buying Prepress

Before buying prepress you need to consider a number of factors. Start with all of the previous issues. Since so much about image reproduction is subjective, it is important that you satisfy yourself that the quality you will obtain is likely to meet your expectations. Subjective issues are hard to argue about after the event, particularly since results that are unacceptable to one person may be quite acceptable to another. So you must ensure that the supplier can achieve what you expect. If you have not used them before, ensure that they can produce what you want either by looking at other work they have done or get them to undertake test pages selected to show the likely problems. As discussed previously, if you are considering buying your own equipment, which many buyers now do for the scanning and page assembly, evaluate it using suitable test procedures prior to purchase. And if you are likely to have a high throughput, don't forget the productivity issues. Ensure you time all the tests.

Once you have confirmed that your likely suppliers can achieve what you require in terms of quality, you now need to consider the specification to go with the order and the copy. The information required by the prepress suppliers follow.

Scanning and color separation. The information required for scanning is the final size, orientation for the scan, the scan rate required, the file format and media required by the next person in the production chain, the color space in which it should be encoded, and any special instructions concerning color and spatial reproduction (such as "open up the highlights or shadows," "clean it up," "match a special color," or "soften/sharpen it"). Terms like these in common use can be somewhat ambiguous, so try to give concrete examples if you can, such as previous work, or talk it over very carefully with the supplier. The good news is that you have the proofing cycle to correct it if things go wrong; the bad news is that it is likely to cost you.

The color separator needs to know the file format and media required for the separated image, as well as the file format of the image being received and a specification for the printing and/or proofing process that is to be used (see proofing section). He or she may be tagging the images with the screening information, and if so will need to know what screening parameters to use, as well as any total dot percentage limit that will define the UCR/GCR levels. You also need to specify which of these two options for achieving the dot percentage you will require. Again any special color and spatial reproduction requirements need to be stated as well as any dot area limits in the highlights and shadows (maximum and minimum reproducible dot percent age).

Page assembly. The same format and media information will be needed for page make-up as for separation (what will be received and what needs to be returned) as well as the obvious things such as layout, page size, bleeds, choke and spread requirements, screening details and fonts required.

Output to film or plate. The output service will need to know the file format and color space the image is encoded in, together with any screening information, and possibly additional information such as whether the films or plates should be negative or positive, and whether the films should be right or wrong reading at a specified emulsion position (up or down), the required density of the image and nonimage areas, dot fringe width (dot hardness), image size tolerance (separation-to-separation and overall) and, if making final pressready films or plates, the imposition requirements (including scheme, gutters, grip, shingling, and margins), and the cut, registration and fold mark requirements and color bar details.

Proofing. For digital proofing, the supplier will also need to know the file format and color space the image is encoded in, and any screening information. Both analog and digital proofing suppliers will need a specification of the printing process they are simulating, a sample of the substrate to show its color and gloss, the ink color required, the dot gain for at least five points in the scale (typically 5%, 25%, 50%, 75% and 95% dot), some registration definition and the number of proofs required.

This list may seem a bit daunting, and it is. Fortunately, for many of the printing processes, the process control parameters have been standardized. Various bodies such as individual publishers, FOGRA, Pira, FIPP and SWOP have done this piecemeal over the years but now it is being brought together by ISO under a standard known as ISO 12647—process control for the manufacture of halftone color separations, proofs, and production prints. Work is at various stages in defining five parts to this standard:

- Part 1 defines the principles, parameters and measurement methods
- Part 2 defines the offset process on a number of different substrates (and thereby encompasses SWOP and FIPP)
- Part 3 defines coldset offset and letterpress on newsprint
- Part 4 defines gravure

- Part 5 defines screen printing

Flexo is still pending. Thus a print buyer can simply refer to one of these and thereby avoid individual definitions for many of the items listed above.

Standards and Their Relevance to the Print Buyer

Turning to the work of the standards bodies provides the conclusion for this chapter. It is the introduction of standards *(defacto* or *dejure)* that makes efficient production possible in an open environment and so the print buyer should be aware of them and how they can be used. The range of areas in which standardization has occurred is so large that in this section we can do no more than indicate the main points of importance to the graphic arts industry. However, these should be adequate for most print buyers.

Defacto standards such as PostScript and TIFF have already been discussed, and both of these have now evolved into *dejure* ISO standards. Another *defacto* standard that looks likely to do the same is the ICC color profile specification, which enables effective information exchange between color management systems. It is not necessary for the user to know anything about the details of these standards; that is for vendors. However, he or she should know of their existence and when to specify their use.

In fact many useful standards start as industry specifications. Bodies such as SWOP and FIPP were formed because of the realization that magazine production relied on a variety of advertisers producing color separations for inclusion in the different magazines. Without some specification for these separations, consistent reproduction of all advertisements was impossible when ganged together on the printing press. Such specifications were then developed for printing processes, rather than products, by bodies such as FOGRA and these are now being given the authority of full standards by the ISO. As mentioned before, a range of standards have been developed for printing process control under ISO 12647. Buyers should be aware of those appropriate to their needs and make use of them in specifications. By doing so, it will become possible to choose from a greater range of producers.

However, other important standards came about more directly. The standards for the color of process inks, ISO 2846, were established by investigating the colors in common use internationally and producing a standard that provided the "center" of these. These are of importance to the buyer only indirectly; the derivative standards described in the previous paragraph cover all that is needed.

The standards for viewing conditions are more important directly. Communication of color relies on either measurement or visual assessment. At present for matching images across media it is difficult to rely on measurement alone. Thus the standard ISO 3664, which is currently under revision, is necessary to ensure consistent viewing and should be used by all concerned.

Other standards of interest and importance to the print buyer are the set of test images for evaluation and setup of output devices (ISO 12640), various test images for setting up color scanners and their color management profiles (ISO 12641 and 12642), platemaking procedures (ISO 12218) and measurement standards for color (ISO 13655) and density (ISO 5–1, 5–2, 5–3, and 13656). Standards under discussion that may be relevant to print buyers include those for the setup and viewing of color monitors, control of direct-to-plate exposure systems, and calibration devices for measuring halftone images by density.

One of the problems with the standards process is the relatively slow pace of development. This is becoming more significant given the rate of change of the technology and so the ISO process is attempting to speed up. Nevertheless, it is true that the process can often be too slow to really meet the needs of the industry. This is why the development of defacto standards is so important since they can (sometimes) be much faster. The later ratification by ISO can then also be a procedure whereby some of the major problems get removed and the process becomes much tighter. The indications are that the PostScript and TIFF ratifications are achieving removal of some of the inconsistencies.

However, such standards will only be useful if they are widely implemented. Often the user community has to demand this to push vendors into doing it, since they are the ones with the practical need. It is important for users to be aware of the developments, and, where appropriate and useful, demand the introduction of them in the products they buy. Where such standards do not meet the needs of users, they should provide their input to the national standards bodies, such as ANSI in the U.S. and BSI in the U.K.

9 Proofing

Phil Green

The proof has a critical role to play in the approval cycle for a printing job, in that it is the means by which approval can be given for a stage in the production process so that it is possible to continue to the next step. It is used to prevent errors appearing in the finished job and to ensure that the final job reflects the client's intentions as closely as possible.

As well as providing a means of giving approval for work already carried out, the proof acts as a guide to the printer showing what the customer wants the job to look like. The press operator, for example, mounts it on the press console during the production run and endeavors to ensure that each printed copy matches it.

The proof also gives important feedback on the production process, both in terms of the current job and also (more generally) on the way that the process is set up (for example, whether high dot gain levels are being experienced).

It is possible to proof every single stage of production, and for each stage to have several iterations of proof and correction until the work done is approved. For some high-value work this is indeed done, but the actual number of proofs that are made for any job will depend on its value and complexity, and the magnitude of the loss that could be incurred through producing a substandard finished product.

As a minimum, a proof will be needed for the design phase and for the production phase of the job. The design proof or visual is aimed at gaining client approval for the design of the job before it goes into production, while the final production proof or contract proof is intended to demonstrate that all the prepress work has been carried out correctly and that the finished job will be acceptable to the client. The design visual will often involve several iterations to establish the client's requirements before final approval of the design is given; but the contract proof is produced to demonstrate that the production process has produced the correct result, and the aim is to get it right first time.

The contract proof, as its name suggests, forms a part of the contract between the buyer and the supplier. It is a record of what the buyer has agreed to pay for and the printer has agreed to produce. Depending on the nature of the contract, both parties may be bound by this agreement.

Requirements of Proofs

To play its role in the approval cycle the proof should be able to simulate the final printed result with an acceptable degree of realism. It should also be cost effective to produce, especially where multiple proofs are needed, and should be sufficiently quick to make sure that it does not delay production.

In the case of the contract proof, its ability to simulate the final printed result (including aspects like color, resolution, and halftoning) is of critical importance. There can also be an issue of acceptability with proofing systems, with some clients unwilling or unable to interpret what the job will look like after seeing a proof on, for example, special proofing paper instead of the paper being used for the job, or with a high gloss level from a laminate proof system.

Design visuals have quite different requirements from contract proofs. Since their purpose is to determine the best way of satisfying the client's needs through successive iterations they should be fast and economical to make, but do not normally need to have such a high degree of fidelity to the final printed result. Increasingly the need for real-time corrections and alterations and fast transmission of corrected proofs makes soft proofing (viewing pages on-screen without a printed copy) a useful proofing medium.

Contract proofs, on the other hand, commit both the client and the printer to the final appearance of the printed product. It must be emphasized that the role of the proof is to show the result that will be achieved when the job is printed, under normal printing conditions, not to set a target for the printer to meet regardless of the difficulty involved.

Contract proofs inevitably cost more and take longer to produce than visuals. Soft proofing is less acceptable for approval of color as there is no permanent record of what was approved.

The contract proof can be produced at different stages in the production workflow, either from the printing plates (wet proofs), from film (prepress proofs) or from the job files (digital proofs). These three types of proof are discussed in more detail later in this chapter.

Changes in Proofing

Both the role and methods of proofing are undergoing radical changes alongside the changes in print production. Developments in proofing technologies have made new methods of proofing available to the buyer, especially in the digital proofing area, and these developments have accompanied changes in workflow with the move towards electronic prepress and the client taking control of more stages in production.

Shorter production lead times also demand changes in the approval process. Improvements in print quality that have resulted from both client demand and advances in printing technology have emphasized the need for consistency and accuracy in proofing. At the same time, pressure to reduce print costs has forced many printers and their clients to reevaluate the cost of proofing and look for possible savings.

Cost of Proofing

Proofs are a significant part of the overall cost of the job. While it is acknowledged that it can be a false economy to dispense with them altogether, since they do not actually contribute any value to the final product, they must be seen as a legitimate target for cost reduction.

Some publishers have taken this approach to the logical conclusion of eliminating all editorial proofs after initial laser proofs of assembled pages (retaining proofs of advertising matter), and are making substantial annual savings as a result.

Some strategies that can aid in reducing the cost of proofing are:

- Plan the approval cycle to use the smallest number of proofs possible after initial visuals. This will keep down the cost of proofs and the time spent on checking them.
- Control alteration costs — make sure that, as far as possible, all changes are made at the appropriate stage in production, the later an alteration is made the more it will cost.
- Always use the cheapest available method of approval, for example, when making a text change after color has been approved, it should not be necessary to see another color proof in order to approve the text alteration — a laser proof or a mono prepress proof should suffice.

- Consider soft proofing where appropriate, as the cost of proofing and correction are lower than with hard copy techniques.
- Do not expect to pay for reproofs if the first proof was not a reasonable representation of your job.
- Get estimates on alternative proofing methods, for single proofs, prepress proofing systems are invariably cheaper than press proofs; yet for multiple copies of proofs, press proofs tend to cost less than other systems.

Printers now have much better process control and work to tighter tolerances than previously, and it is now possible to shift the focus of approval upstream to the design and prepress phases of production, reducing to a minimum the number of proofs that are made after the job has gone into production. If the prepress proofing system can accurately simulate the printing process, and the process is controlled to known standards, then the variation between proof and print should be very small. This makes it possible to treat the design visual as a production prototype, with no further proofing needed in all but the most demanding of work.

The Approval Cycle

The approval cycle has been discussed in Chapter 1, and the proof is both the mechanism by which approval can take place and the physical evidence that documents it.

As with the approval cycle in general, it is important to establish the degree of formality and traceability that is needed in proofing. Informal communications with suppliers may be largely by word of mouth, and are often extremely successful when they work on the basis of a high degree of trust and mutual understanding. On more complex projects, when more people are involved, or with suppliers that you have not yet built up a relationship with, there tends to be a need for a more formal approach to proofing and correction. The aim of more formal systems is to create systems that work independently of the personalities involved, eliminate ambiguities in communication, and provide evidence of what has been agreed.

More formal approval methods are often just good practice, but moving to them should be done with care. They should be introduced in a coherent way rather than as a piecemeal response to individual problems, and they must be maintained consistently or they will be ignored.

The main points of a documented system are:
- Deciding on who will be responsible for what aspects of approval during the planning of a job (with a schedule if possible)
- Agreeing on the terminology to be used, including the proof correction symbols and the terms for marking up color corrections
- Keeping records, including copies of all approved or corrected proofs with a note of who was responsible;
- Making sure that each proof is dated and each iteration is given a version number
- Approving each element of a job once only

The last three points form the basis of a proofing audit trail, by which it is possible to check back through a set of proofs to identify when specific changes were made and by whom. The final point — approving each element no more than once — also avoids the common problem whereby a page is approved with some minor alteration, but it is later found that some other aspect of the page has been changed as well (and naturally will not have been noticed on the reproof as it will not have been the item being checked). The actual items being approved should be clearly identified to suppliers, and if necessary items should be struck through on a reproof to indicate that they have been previously approved. Then it is the supplier's responsibility to check for internal errors that result in unforeseen changes.

Note that a documented system does not automatically require hard-copy proofs, and several soft proofing methods (such as Adobe Acrobat) allow you to save the necessary information with the file.

A valuable technique that can be implemented when more than one person is involved in the approval process is to set up a checklist of items to approve. This helps to ensure that things are not overlooked, and can give confidence that even the more inexperienced members of your team will be able to take responsibility for proof correction.

Ideally, the approval cycle is planned to ensure that corrections happen in a timely fashion, but in the real world it is common for alterations to be made even at a late stage in production. The approval cycle has to accommodate this reality while attempting to minimize the costs of such changes.

The earlier in the production workflow that the proof is made, the lower any correction or alteration costs will be, but at the same time the poorer the simulation of the final result will be and the greater the degree of interpretation called for.

The choice of proofing system is determined largely by the approval cycle, taking into consideration factors such as the subject matter and the production stage that requires approval.

Proofing Technologies

Proofs used as visuals in design and the early parts of prepress are intended to show the position and color of text and graphic elements, although they are not usually expected to represent the exact appearance of colors, text weights, or tint values. The contract proof, on the other hand, must portray these accurately and consistently as they will appear on the final job. The factors that will affect this are:

- The facility to calibrate the proofing system to give the same dot gain as the printing process
- The ability to use the same paper stock that will be used in the final job
- The ability to use special colors in addition to the four-color process set
- The resolution capability of the proofing system
- The type of colorants used, and how close their appearance is to that of the printing inks
- The level of gloss in the proof, and the ability to reduce the gloss of laminate proofs to emulate the printing process
- The method of halftoning used
- The ability to render accurately all the graphic elements in the job in the same way as the RIP, used in the output device, and in film exposure and platesetting.

Calibration. It is essential to calibrate the proofing system to match the printing process. There is an enormous variation in the amount of dot gain experienced in different processes, ranging from dot gain in the midtones of under 16% in sheetfed offset on coated stock to around 50% in flexo on newsprint. Dot gain must be accurate to between 1–2% to avoid significant discrepancies between proof and print.

PMS colors. PMS colors are limited to press proofs and a small number of other proofing systems, such as Cromalin and Matchprint prepress proofs and inkjet digital proofing systems. If a PMS color is unavailable, it is necessary to substitute one of the process colors or produce a separate mono proof of the PMS color. In practice many smaller suppliers do not have the facilities to apply PMS colors, although the materials are readily available from the proofing system vendors (for example, many repro houses are not familiar with the Pantone range of toners for Cromalin proofs, but DuPont will be happy to supply them). If a supplier has to buy materials for proofing PMS colors, they may make an additional charge.

Substrates. Restricting the choice of proofing substrates makes it difficult to capture the precise look and feel of the finished job, especially when uncoated or mechanical papers are to be used. Many prepress and digital proofing systems, including DuPont Cromalin, Kodak Signature, and the Iris and Digital Cromalin inkjet systems, are able to image onto printing papers. Again, smaller suppliers may be unfamiliar with the methods for proofing onto printing papers, but can obtain the information from the proofing system vendor.

Inks. Printing inks contain a blend of pigments, varnishes, and resins that give a characteristic appearance to printed color. The pigments used determine the color gamut (the range of colors that can be printed) of the process, while the resins and varnishes determine the gloss and smoothness; ideally both should be closely matched by the proofing system. Other colorants such as toners and photographic emulsions cannot simulate the effect of printing inks exactly, although in some cases the difference is negligible.

Gloss. Gloss is a property of the paper used for the job, as well as the inks and finishes employed. A common problem with proofing systems, especially those that are based on multiple laminates such as Cromalin, is that the gloss of the proof is much higher than the final print. If the client is unable to make allowances for this effect they may have unrealistic expectations of what the final job will look like. Cromalin and Matchprint proofing systems provide a means of matte finishing the proof to reduce the gloss to a more realistic level.

Resolution. The resolution of prepress proofs is the same as the film they are made from, and so will match that of the print. However, with a few exceptions, digital proofing systems image the proofing substrate differently from the final output to film or plate, and as a result they have a lower resolution than the final print. This will make the proof look less sharp and make fine lines and type, in smaller sizes, look poor. Most digital proofing systems incorporate some method of varying the density of the colorant. This does offset the lower resolution capability in the case of images, although type and graphics still suffer. An alternative approach (adopted by Kodak's Approval and Optronics' Intelliproof systems) is to image the proof by laser, which achieves a resolution as great as (or close to) that of the film or plate output device.

Halftoning is particularly affected by the resolution of the proofing system, and for digital proofs only the laser-imaging systems can replicate halftone dots accurately. Dye sublimation devices do not use any form of halftoning, relying instead on their ability to image varying densities of colorant to render tone. Inkjet proofing devices either print an approximation of halftone dots (Iris) or use FM screening (Digital Cromalin).

It is useful to be able to see the halftone dot structure on the proof, to check for artifacts such as *moiré* patterns, but given the technical difficulties in imaging halftone dots on digital proofs, it is probably advisable to do this on a prepress or press proof if it is absolutely necessary.

Rendering all the graphic elements of a job, particularly items such as overprints and traps, is not done consistently on all output devices. This can lead to such problems as objects appearing to be masked on a digital proof but then imaging correctly on the film output device (or vice versa). This is a limitation of the rips built into digital proofing devices, but one which is being addressed by the device manufacturers.

The size of the proof should ideally be able to include at least two 8.5×11-in. pages to view, with room for bleeds, trim, and register marks and control strips. If imposed flats are to be checked the proof will need to be much larger, usually on the same size as the sheet being printed. Few prepress suppliers have machines of this size, restricting large-format proofs to press proofs.

There are three basic methods of making a proof:
- From the printing plates (known as press proofs or wet proofs)

- From the films that will be used to make the plates (referred to as analog prepress proofs or photomechanical proofs)
- From the digital data that will be used to output the films (known as digital proofs)

In the case of digital proofs, they may be in the form of hard copy imaged by a digital printing device, or they may be viewed on screen as soft proofs.

Press Proofs

Press proofs, being made from the plates that will be used in the production run, have the advantage of being capable of reproducing the printed image just as it will appear in the final job, although in reality the greater human element involved means that there is a degree of inconsistency in the results achieved. Press proofs can be made on special proofing presses (fast to set up but slow to run), or, for even greater fidelity to the printing process, on a production press. The latter are often referred to as machine proofs; the press can be set up just to run the proof, after which the plates are lifted and the proof sent to the client for approval, or alternatively the client may be present to approve the job at the beginning of the production run, in which case it is known as a pass-on-press.

The advantage of machine proofing is that it achieves the greatest fidelity to the final result, although it is more costly to implement. Alterations are expensive when compared to other methods of proofing, particularly in the case of the pass-on-press, where plates must be lifted and the job rescheduled. Realistically the pass-on-press is limited to fine-tuning the amount of ink being run, all approval of content having being carried out at an earlier stage.

The type of thing that a press proof will show that will not appear on other types of proof include:
- The effect of tracking (the influence on the inking caused by other pages or other objects in the same machine direction—for example, a heavy black solid tracking with an image would tend to lead to over-inking of the image)
- The content of the job exactly as it will appear on the final print, including halftones and solid color overprints
- The consequence of paper properties such as stretch and absorbency (leading to effects such as misregister and mottle)

A common problem arising from the use of proof presses is that the operator may fail to match the characteristics of the production press. Proof presses are capable of much higher inking levels and sharper halftones than production presses, and it is quite easy to produce a proof that cannot be matched when the job is eventually printed.

Prepress Proofs

Analog prepress proofs are the most widely used method of proofing since (for most types of work) their speed, consistency and economy outweighs their inability to produce an exact match to the printing process. They are mostly made by exposing films to light-sensitive materials which are then colored, usually requiring a separate laminate layer for each color.

Analog proofing systems have only a limited ability to match process characteristics such as dot gain. Vendors have developed techniques for at least partially overcoming these limitations, and it is possible to produce a good match for the visual appearance if not the feel of a printed job with several systems such as DuPont Cromalin, Konica Konsensus, 3M Matchprint and Kodak Signature, all of which have gained wide acceptance as contract proofs. (Signature is infrequently encountered outside the publication printing sector, where it has built up a reputation for producing a good match to the print on a wide range of magazine paper qualities.)

Digital Proofs

Digital proofs are made from the page data before the films are output. They are a much newer technology than analog and press proofing, and have yet to gain universal acceptance. However, their advantages are likely to make them the dominant proofing method before long. The main reason for this is the shift in working methods with traditional prepress increasingly being carried out by designers and publishers. Once all the elements of a page have been assembled in a page make-up application it is then possible to generate a proof, and delaying it until a later stage in production only increases the consequent alteration costs. In addition, a digital proof is cheaper than the alternatives, and while a close match to the final print is not possible with all devices, the ability to precisely calibrate output, coupled with developments in imaging technology, will remove the main objections that remain.

A major barrier to acceptance of digital proofs as contract proofs is the reluctance of printers to be contractually bound to match a proof where there is no assurance that the proof has been produced to the same standards that they work to. This issue is being addressed by the use of digital control strips that allow the printer to measure characteristics such as dot gain and confirm that the proof is acceptable, in the same way that they can test a press or prepress proof.

A further point is that both the proofing device and the device which will image the films or plates must both work to the same standard and must be accurately calibrated, or there will be an additional source of variation between proof and print.

Soft proofing is growing rapidly in some sectors of the industry as it takes the arguments in favor of digital proofing a stage further. Simply previewing individual elements or complete pages on screen is the easiest method of soft proofing, but since designers are usually unwilling to allow access to job files owing to the risk that a client might attempt to edit them, or take them away and place the work elsewhere, file previewing has a number of limitations:

- The client has no record of what was approved.
- For photographic images the low-resolution previews in an image file are inadequate for approval purposes and the alternative of viewing the high-resolution image is time-consuming owing to the large file size.
- There is no straightforward way of marking up a graphic or assembled page (as opposed to editing it).

Moreover, it is often impractical for the client to travel to the designer to see a screen preview, especially given the increasing trend for client and supplier to be remote from each other. Transferring files for approval causes a separate set of problems: they can take too long to transfer electronically, storage media are costly and can give rise to compatibility problems, and the client may not have the necessary software to open the files, or may be using a different hardware platform.

Clearly the need is for a platform-independent, portable file format that does not contain high-resolution information, but otherwise shows the appearance of the page accurately and can be annotated. There are several competing technologies, but the most successful is Adobe Acrobat. Acrobat is a subset of the PostScript page description language. As such can be relied upon to render page elements faithfully just as they would be on a PostScript output device. Acrobat viewers are freely available for most hardware platforms, and Acrobat printer drivers that generate Acrobat files can be used in conjunction with most graphics applications including Illustrator, PageMaker, and QuarkXPress, making it very easy to create an Acrobat file from the completed pages. By using additional software in the form of Acrobat Exchange, customers can annotate the proof directly and return it. It is possible to transmit just the annotations to avoid the need to return the entire file.

An alternative approach used by advertising agencies, among others, is to have a proofing device (either a digital printer or a calibrated monitor) at the client's premises which is online to the prepress supplier. A proof can be downloaded to this device and viewed by the client, who can discuss it with the prepress system operator over the phone. Corrections can also be returned immediately by fax or email. This permits repeated iterations in a short space of time and is highly effective when quality requirements are high and deadlines are tight. The main drawback to this approach is the cost of the system, and print buyers should ensure that any equipment installed for this purpose is not restricted to working with a single supplier.

Proof Markup   Carefully marking up proofs with corrections and alterations is one of the principal means by which the print buyer ensures that the final printed product conforms with the requirements of the job and has the maximum value to the client. However, it is important not to lose sight of the main objective of the approval process, which is to reach a point where a job can be approved for production. This should be achieved as efficiently as possible.

In many cases more than one person is involved in checking proofs, and to assist the printer to interpret your changes it is essential to arrive at some consistency of mark-up procedure. This implies using language unambiguously and consistently, and employing standard proof correction marks where possible. It is also important to identify the people who should see a proof of a job, ensuring that they receive it at the appropriate stage in production, and to clarify their responsibility in the approval process. Checklists are a useful tool to aid in this process. The proof should be circulated, with the checklist, and a copy of the proof correction symbols if the recipients do not already possess them.

When several people are expected to correct a proof, it is often helpful if everyone uses a different color of pen to mark their corrections. You can prevent the proof becoming a tangle of competing (or even conflicting) instructions by giving them overlay sheets to write corrections on that can be combined later.

When viewing a proof, the items that are to be approved can be grouped into three headings: position, color, and content.

When checking content it is important to look for output errors such as text reflows, font substitutions, incorrect or absent traps, (see Chapter 7 for more information on these aspects) as well as confirming that the content is all present and appears as it did on the original copy.

For appraising color proofs, it is essential to view the proof under standard viewing conditions. Specified colors (both PMS colors and CMYK tints) should be checked against printed samples (such as Pantone swatches and process color tint charts). Control strips are useful to determine whether the proof has been made to the appropriate standard and will, as a result, be possible for the printer to match.

Checking position involves checking the color registration of the whole sheet and the fit of individual elements; other items to check include the way in which the elements butt up together, the matching up of spreads across folds, and the accuracy of any tint laying that has been done. It is also important to check that the page size is correct and that individual elements have been cropped and scaled correctly.

Standard proof correction marks for text are specified in ANSI Z39.22 and ISO 5776. Corrections to graphics have been standardized in some countries (such as the U.K.), but most correction systems for graphics and images are based on company guidelines instead of national ones.

Proofing for Computer-to-Plate and Computer-to-Press

Digital production technologies that eliminate the film stage make it impossible to use the usual film-based proofing systems such as Cromalin, unless film is generated solely for the purpose of making a proof — clearly a wasteful process. In a computer-to-press environment it is more economical to prepare the press and run a machine proof than it would be with conventional printing, but it is still more costly than prepress proofing.

Digital proofing methods are the only feasible method of proofing for direct digital output cost-effectively, but in situations where there is not enough confidence in the veracity of the digital proofing systems available, there may be no alternative but to generate film. In some cases it may be appropriate to use a digital proofing medium that can be imaged in the imagesetter (such as Optronics' Intelliproof) as this will at least ensure that the same raster image is marked on both proof and plate.

10 The Printing Processes

Kelvin Tritton, David Atkinson,
John Stephens, and Phil Green

This chapter describes the developments in the four major printing processes — offset lithography, flexography, gravure, screen process — together with the more recent digital printing technologies. Each process is undergoing development and innovation that can add value to the printed product, either by enhancing the perceived quality of the product, or by making it cheaper or faster to produce. Some of the innovations described do more than merely improve existing products; they make it possible for the specifier or designer to create an entirely new product.

Lithographic Printing
Kelvin Tritton

During recent years, we have seen litho printing responding to the demands for shorter run lengths and more rapid change-over, while also maintaining and improving print quality and reducing waste. These continue to be the forces driving current developments in litho printing.

Sheetfed Litho Presses

Developments concentrate on the reduction in changeover time rather than increased production speeds. The maximum production speed for medium-format presses has reached a plateau at 15,000 sheets per hour (sph), with some large presses and perfectors having a maximum speed of 12,000 sph. The predicted demise of small offset presses in the face of competition from digital printing systems is now being reflected in the new equipment available. Even the GTO 52, which has been the backbone of many small- and medium-size printers, is now showing its age with respect to the features found on modern sheetfed presses, such as automatic plateloading, automatic cleaning, automatic changeover from straight printing to perfecting, and remote adjustment of register. It is clearly Heidelberg's intention that it will be replaced by the Speedmaster 52 in the future.

The main press manufacturers now offer eight-unit sheetfed presses with the ability to print straight or perfecting. There are also reported installations of ten-unit presses. For the print buyer, this means that there will be an increase in the availability of presses to print those jobs that have previously required two or more press passes. More printers will be keen to exploit the capability to print hi-fi color. Others may provide a more cost-effective option to web, for the production of short-run color magazine type products, on these presses when used in a perfecting mode.

The large-format (e.g., 40×56-in.) sheetfed presses have not, until now, offered the improvements in automated setup and higher running speed found on the medium-format presses. The recently launched Roland 900 and the KBA Rapida 142 are both highly automated and print at speeds unobtainable on the large format presses of the past.

The market for very-large-format presses is obviously not as great as for the medium-format (e.g., 28×40–ιv.) presses, but there are many carton and book printers who use this format and will now be able to gain significant improvements in productivity as a result of this press development. They have in the past predominantly used the Roland 800, which has a maximum production speed of only 10,000 and makeready times normally between one and two hours. It should certainly be possible to achieve makeready within 30 minutes with the automated plate changer on these presses.

Computer-to-Press

Heidelberg launched the Quickmaster-DI, its replacement for the GTO-DI, in 1995. This press utilizes the latest development of Presstek's waterless plate in a press designed specifically to exploit this market sector. No longer is it necessary to change plates manually upon completion of a job. The plate material is a continuous length (35 repeats) that is wound from one spool to another after the completion of each job. The print quality is also significantly improved on that of the early GTO-DI.

The changeover from one job to the next will typically take between 10 and 20 minutes, depending on imaging resolution. The plates are claimed to have a run length capability of up to 20,000 copies. Installation began during 1996.

Digital printing systems such as Indigo's E-Print 1000 and Agfa's Chromapress are generally accepted to offer the most

economical cost per copy for quantities below 500, but a significant proportion of short run color printing requires run lengths in the 1000 to 3000 category. Companies installing the Quickmaster-DI should give the print buyer the opportunity to purchase color print in this category at a competitive cost.

Web Presses

The emphasis for web press developments is similar to that for sheetfed presses but unlike sheetfed, production speeds continue to increase significantly. Web offset competes with sheetfed at the lower run lengths. Therefore, quick change-over and low waste are important. But at the other end the competition is gravure, where high production speeds are an important factor. Therefore the press developments reflect the need to compete in both of these markets.

Automatic or semi-automatic plate loading is now offered on many new presses, and this can reduce job-change to less than 20 minutes if there is no folder change or if this is also automated. This, coupled with the reduced paper waste that comes from more accurate plate location and pre-setting, lowers the run lengths that are viable for web production.

Much of the recent discussion associated with web press developments is suffixed with "less," for example: gapless, pinless, shaftless and waterless. "Gapless" refers to the blanket cylinder having no gap. The blanket is a replaceable

Figure 10-2.
The Heidelberg Harris
"Sunday Press."

sleeve. The Heidelberg Harris M-3000 "Sunday Press" was the first web press of this generation to have gapless blanket cylinders.

The absence of a gap eliminates the mechanical disturbances, which on conventional presses have an adverse influence on print quality when printing at high speed. By reducing or eliminating the nonprinting gap, the production speed and web width of the press can be increased. The cutoff is also reduced while still allowing the same size product to be produced, but the benefit of this can only be exploited to the fullest if the space required for the traditional folder pin holes can be avoided. This is achieved if the press is fitted with a "pinless" folder.

The benefits of this technology are mainly applicable in the longer run magazine and catalog market, with run lengths in excess of 250,000. The print quality achieved with a 1:1 gapless press is likely to suffer less from the compromises that can apply with a 2:1 designed web press, but the signature sizes are smaller and this can increase the demands and costs in finishing.

The term "shaftless" relates to the fact that traditionally, the drive of printing units, chill rolls and the folder have been linked by a drive shaft. The Heidelberg Harris M-3000 and others have a fully digitally controlled drive system with no drive shaft. This isolates torsional disturbances and reduces the number of mechanical parts. In general there are significant benefits to be gained from this system of press drive, and it is likely to be a common feature of web press design in the future, but it has no direct consequences for the print buyer.

"Waterless" is no longer solely the preserve of web printing, as most of the more recently designed sheetfed presses have provision or option for ink system cooling. This means that there are generally no significant obstacles to prevent a printer from adopting waterless production, if the work and economics make this a sensible choice. There are few web offset installations dedicated to waterless printing outside of Japan; it is not, therefore, an option that can be considered by most print buyers at this time. However, increased interest is being shown in the possibilities of exploiting the low start-up waste associated with waterless, combined with quick job change-over opportunities afforded by automatic plate changing, to produce web runs below 50,000.

A further significant increase in the volume of waterless printing is very dependent on the availability of competitive products. The anticipated competition to Toray in the plate market is still awaited.

Flexographic Printing
David Atkinson

Flexography is the last of the major mechanical printing processes to reach maturity and is still in a phase of rapid development, with optimum print quality potential yet to be achieved within most of the flexographic print markets. Demands from print buyers for flexographic printing comparable to that produced by litho and gravure, coupled with ongoing developments in presses and printing materials, are driving flexographic printers to strive for constant improvements in print quality.

In today's highly competitive environment, price is a major deciding factor when purchasing print, and this is an area where flexography can always compete favorably with other processes. Flexography is basically a simple process with the ability to convert most printed materials in-line and this, along with fairly low repro costs, makes it very cost effective. Flexographic presses are a lower capital investment than a comparable size of webfed lithographic or gravure press and running costs are also lower. Flexographic origination costs are much lower than those for gravure, and scrap levels are much less than those for litho. This intrinsic cost-effectiveness, along with constantly improving quality, has for many years now facilitated a growth in market share. Flexography is currently the only one of the major mechanical processes still increasing its market share and is, more importantly, still entering previously untapped markets.

The majority of flexographic presses are webfed, the only sheetfed products being directly printed corrugated board and some envelopes. The process is extremely versatile and is capable of printing on virtually any material, including papers, boards, films, foils and laminates. Depending on the press, it is possible to print carton board up to 0.04 inch (1 mm) thick and films just a few microns thick. This versatility makes it possible to print a very wide range of products.

Historically, flexography developed as a package printing process and is still used predominantly for the printing of packaging materials. In recent years, however, it has entered the field of publication work and is now also used for printing newsprint, comics, paperbacks, and telephone directories. At present, 47 daily newspapers in North America are printed (at least partially) using flexography, with another 75 expected to add flexo technology in the near future. With paper prices escalating, flexographic print technology improving, and environmental concerns increasing, flexography is now a much more attractive option than it was a few years ago, when the last major investment in newsprint took place upon the demise of letterpress. When compared with lithography for newspaper production, flexography offers the advantage of lower capital equipment costs, reduced energy consumption, environmentally friendly water-based inks with no rub-off, brighter colors, and greatly reduced scrap levels.

One perceived disadvantage of flexographic newsprint is that of recycling. When mixed newsprint waste containing a high percentage of flexographic waste is dealt with using the conventional flotation technique, it is difficult to achieve an acceptable degree of brightness due to the flexographic pigment size. However, this problem could be resolved by using other recycling techniques or segregating waste.

Other flexographically printed products include corrugated containers, folding cartons, liquid packaging, flexible packaging such as freezer bags and potato chip bags, wrapping paper, tissue paper, wall coverings, paper bags, multi-wall sacks, plastic carrier bags, cups, closures, tickets, tags, labels, forms and envelopes. Flexography has almost 100% share of the multi-wall sack, direct-printed corrugated container, and tissue paper print markets. In other print markets flexography competes with the other printing processes for business, and any increase in flexographic market share is often at the expense of the other processes.

One of the latest markets to open up for flexography is that of small-format folding cartons; gains in this market will be at the expense of lithography and gravure. It is less than five years since the process first entered this very demanding market, but already some of the best flexographic print quality around can be seen on cartons.

Strengths of the flexographic process, when compared with lithography, are superior metallics and strong dense solids. The basic nature of the flexographic printing plates and inks make it difficult to achieve fine vignettes, very light tones, shadow detail and small typefaces reversed out of dense solids. Controlling these aspects is the key to achieving high-quality, consistent flexographic printing.

The flexographic printing plate is most commonly a flat, fairly soft, relief plate made from a photopolymer material. One of the problems associated with soft relief printing plates is that they are noncompressible and deform under pressure, giving rise to a "halo" around the image and excessive dot gain. For this reason press settings, printing plate caliper and substrate caliper need to be very carefully controlled if consistent print quality is to be achieved. When these flat relief printing plates are wrapped around a rotary plate cylinder, the image surface elongates, giving rise to potential register problems. Elongation of the plate surface also gives rise to caliper variation. All these effects can be considerably reduced by the use of thinner printing plates, and all sectors of the flexographic printing industry are currently moving towards thinner photopolymer printing plates. Some printers are now using plates as thin as 0.045 in. (1.14 mm). As this shift to thinner plates continues, we should see a further improvement in flexographic print capabilities.

The ink systems used for flexographic printing are, in the main, very low-viscosity, fast-drying solvent- or water-based liquid inks that dry by means of evaporation. If transfer volume is not accurately controlled their low viscosity makes them prone to spread under printing pressure, giving rise to increased dot gain and filling-in of fine reverses. Their fast-drying evaporative nature can cause the ink to dry on the surface of the plate, which also gives rise to dot gain and filling-in of print detail. If the ink viscosity is not closely controlled, evaporation from the ink duct during the press run gives rise to changes in color density. UV inks for flexography do not dry by evaporation and are of a higher viscosity than conventional ink systems so when printers revert to UV inks they are not subject to these problems.

For some of the highest quality flexographic printing applications (such as label and carton printing), UV ink sys-

Figure 10-3.
A flexo press at Pira.

tems are now being used more extensively and development work is currently in progress to extend the use of these inks into wide-web film packaging applications. Wider use of these ink systems will bring about great improvements in the general level of flexographic print quality.

As a process, flexography has special prepress requirements. Artwork has to be "disproportioned" in the machine direction to allow for the stretch that occurs to the plate surface when it is wrapped around the printing cylinder. Suitable dot gain curves, as determined from a press fingerprinting exercise, should be used for the color separations. The screen angles used for the color separations are usually offset by 7.5° to prevent potential screen clash with the engraving angle of the ink metering roll, which is often at 45°. The screen ruling used for flexography is typically between 100 lpi and 150 lpi, with the finest screens being used on labels and cartons and the coarser screens being used on flexible films and preprint liners for corrugated box making.

With a relief printing plate ink is carried on the surface. With a very liquid ink system, there is a tendency, when under printing pressure, for the ink to be squeezed out around the edges of the image, causing dot gain and fill-in of print detail. For this reason it is critical that the minimum volume of ink is transferred and that this volume is accurately metered and evenly distributed. In order to achieve these criteria most modern presses are now fitted with doctor blades and laser-engraved ceramic ink metering rollers known as anilox rollers. The doctor blade scrapes surplus ink from the surface of the roller, and the excellent wear properties of ceramics help to maintain the consistency of volume. The volume of ink carried by the anilox roller is determined by the roller engraving.

By nature, flexography is a cost-effective printing process that is very attractive from the price point of view but, until recently, has not been able to match the kind of print quality that the other processes are able to offer. Now, with modern presses using the latest flexographic printing technology, it is possible to produce consistent high-quality flexography. As the latest technical developments penetrate further into the various sectors of the industry, flexography will be able to offer not only cost-effective products but also enhanced print quality. This will make flexography a more obvious choice and will ensure that the process continues to expand and improve its share of the market in the years to come.

Gravure
Phil Green

The gravure process is used mainly for long-run work in the publication and packaging sectors. Low running costs, long-lasting cylinders, and an ability to print on low grades of paper, combine to make gravure highly competitive on a range of work including magazines, catalogs and flexible packaging, although the high cost of cylinder preparation renders it unsuitable for shorter-run work.

The move away from economy-of-scale purchasing, in which long runs are specified, toward just-in-time production and minimal stock-holding have eroded some of the traditional gravure markets, although innovations in press design and prepress are to some extent countering this tendency.

A major advantage of gravure is its ability to produce good quality color work on very cheap papers such as supercalendered mechanicals. Such papers have a smooth and quite glossy surface, although they have little or no coating. However, gravure is less suitable for coated stocks and it is common for the covers of catalogs and periodicals to be printed litho.

Gravure will also print successfully on a wide range of other substrates such as plastic films and metal foils, the main requirement of the process being a smooth surface to print on.

Gravure inks are similar to flexo inks in that they are liquid inks that dry by evaporation. The process is able to print heavier ink films onto the substrate than both litho and flexo, and this permits a greater tonal range to be printed. As a result contrast is high, and excellent results can be achieved with metallics and fluorescents, and other special inks that require a heavy ink film for maximum effect.

However, the solvents used in gravure inks are more volatile than those used in flexo, resulting in levels of VOC emissions that are no longer permitted in most countries. It has been difficult to formulate water-based inks for many gravure applications, and the only successful alternative is for the printer to invest in closed solvent-recovery systems.

In publication gravure, it is common for the presses to have a large number of printing units, making high paginations and multiple colors possible. In addition, cylinders can be produced to any diameter, giving a flexible cutoff (unlike the predetermined cutoff imposed by the fixed diameter of web offset presses), and a wider range of product sizes.

Most of the press developments in recent years have been aimed at reducing makeready times. The main innovation has been the introduction of swing-away cartridges on which the cylinder for the next job can be set up while another job is still running.

In the packaging field, hybrid presses integrating both flexo and gravure units have become popular, and in one design a convertible printing unit allows the printer to switch between the two processes by replacing the flexo anilox and plate cylinders with a gravure cylinder and offset blanket.

There have also been developments in sheetfed gravure presses designed to produce products like labels in shorter runs than are usual for gravure. Other variants of the gravure process (such as pad printing) are used in product decoration units on assembly and packaging lines and in security printing such as checks, postage stamps, and bank notes.

Cylinder Preparation

The image on a gravure cylinder is formed as a pattern of tiny cells recessed into the surface of a cylinder, usually copper-plated, though some manufacturers have introduced ceramic cylinders and polymer sleeves as cheaper alternatives to the expensive copper-plating process. The cylinders are imaged by etching or engraving. Unlike the other conventional processes, these cells can vary in depth and thus print a continuous-tone image. For this reason halftone screens are not required and excellent tonal results can be achieved. However, the cells produce a visible artifact on text, and prints lack the crispness of litho, making gravure more suitable for work where the subject matter is predominantly pictorial.

For publication work, pages can be supplied in exactly the same way as for litho, as page make-up files or as film positives. In traditional electronic engraving, continuous-tone bromides called opalines are made from these and mounted on an electronic scanner. The signals generated by the scanner drive engraving heads (mounted on the copper cylinder) that mechanically peck out cells to the required depth.

In packaging plants the older method of etching cylinders from continuous-tone positives is still in use.

The cost of gravure cylinder production remains a major barrier to its more widespread adoption. Even long runs often include "change plates" for different text editions, and are just as prone to last-minute alterations as any other process. Cylinder cost makes it difficult to accommodate these working practices in gravure, although a countervailing advantage is that gravure print is highly consistent. The cylinders are extremely durable, and as the ink weight is determined by cell depth rather than operator adjustment of ink flow, it is largely unaffected by the inking variations that are common in litho.

The main innovation in cylinder preparation in recent years has been the move towards direct engraving of cylinders from digital data, removing the need to make intermediate films or bromides and then scan them. This has greatly reduced the cost and time involved in cylinder preparation, and allowed gravure printers to work from customer page files in the same way that litho printers do.

Proofs for gravure are usually made using prepress proofing technologies such as Cromalin, although machine proofing may be done for packaging work. The use of digital proofing is increasing owing to its ability to simulate the appearance of gravure printing quite closely.

Screen Process
John Stephens

Screen printing has its origins in a craft-based tradition; this has very much shaped the culture of the industry throughout the world. One of the most significant features of the craft tradition is its emphasis on skilled practice, developed over time and made manifest by a close attention to the quality of practice and product. This has established a work ethic in which pride in the quality of work is a primary motivating force. However, this same craft-based tradition has also placed a high value on the subjective judgment of the experienced and skilled operator. It has also tended to encourage a somewhat conservative attitude toward change. Trust in the tried and tested, and let someone else try the new.

Yet in recent years the rapid developments in screen printing technology have begun to bring about a cultural change in the industry. The advances we are seeing clearly indicate a move away from the craft-based past into the new technological, computer-driven age. Here, the emphasis is upon developing new materials and processes that have pushed forward the quality boundaries of the process. This is especially evident in the areas of four-color process, where developments in screen mesh, stencil systems, ink making, and press design are evident both in the graphic printing and in garment printing sectors.

Screen Mesh and Stencil Materials

Developments in the manufacture of a new high-tech, high-tension polyester screen mesh have brought about increased control parameters in four-color printing that can influence ink deposit, dot formation and dimensional stability of the screen. This development has led directly to increased research into the dynamics of ink transfer that take place during printing. Increased control of the influences of the screen/stencil/off-contact/squeegee pressure dynamic have lead to dramatic improvements in print quality.

Developments in new direct screen imaging emulsions have resulted in high-speed, dual-cure stencil systems for use with screen projection systems for large-format poster and textile printing and for the new inkjet and direct-to-screen laser imaging systems. These developments provide for increased efficiency in prepress, saving on origination costs and providing the customer with faster turnaround.

Ink Systems

Other developments in screen making have focused on the increased drive for water-based ink systems, both conventional drying and UV. Here the concern is to meet the increasing demand for products that meet environmental standards in production. Water-based ink systems have been slow to take off, since they present production problems. However, in a world committed to reducing solvent emissions it is likely that they will continue to be developed and grow more widespread in their application.

Press Design

In recent years developments in press design have focused upon increased automation in makeready systems for two-color press configurations. Svecia, the Swedish machine manufacturer, developed a very effective automatic screen changing mechanism for its two-color high-speed cylinder presses. The system allows two colors to be changed in under one minute.

A number of printers now have four-color presses that utilize flash UV drying systems. This new technology substantially reduces the overall length of the press line and also reduces the energy consumption of the dryer. Rotary screen printing presses for graphic printing (largely narrow-web, label printing presses) have also been developed.

Standardization

There have been concerted efforts to establish an ISO standard for screen printing. This further reflects the move away from the subjective craft-based culture to the new technologically informed culture that fully embraces concepts of systematic quality control based upon the application of technical knowledge, objective measurement and evaluation against established standards.

Much of this work has focused upon establishing a set of production control specifications that relate to variables in the production process, which must be controlled if consistent four-color print reproduction is to be achieved. The application of these standards and the use of color measurement systems commonly used in the other major print processes will further enhance the status of screen printing and increase customer confidence in the wide range of four-color process work that can be produced by the process.

Digital Printing

Phil Green

Digital printing is currently the most rapidly growing print sector, and one which is opening up new possibilities of economical production of short-run color work. It is also enabling entirely different relationships between the purchaser and supplier of printed products and making possible all kinds of new products.

The conventional printing processes described earlier in this chapter are mature technologies. The technological development of these processes will continue, but will tend to deliver only incremental improvements in performance. Digital printing, by comparison, is still at an early stage in its development and will continue to develop rapidly, opening up new markets and making increasing inroads into the conventional processes.

In the medium term at least, it is highly unlikely that digital printing will entirely replace the conventional processes. This is for two fundamental reasons:

- The cost of the colorants used makes unit prices too high to compete on longer runs.
- Modern printing equipment is designed around production economies of scale, with high speeds, large formats and in-line processes such as folding and coating, and it will be some time before manufacturers build digital presses that can compete on high production volumes.

The strength of digital printing is therefore largely in shorter print runs. However, the short-run market is expanding fast as print runs for all types of product are falling, and new products are made possible by integrated digital production. A direct cost comparison between digital and conventional printing may not be relevant in every case as digital printing can often provide a better solution to a communication problem, adding value and generating savings elsewhere in the production cycle, for example, in administration or distribution costs. This logic also applies to the print buyers when thinking of incorporating digital printing into their own operations, adding them to their existing design and prepress operations. To take an example in retailing, in-store printing facilities linked to central price and marketing databases that can produce new point-of-sale materials within minutes may cost more to install and run than purchasing from external suppliers, but the marketing benefits may outweigh the additional costs.

The point at which digital and conventional printing breaks even tends to be at a run length of around 1000 copies (more for black-and-white and less for color). Run lengths that do not fall automatically into the province of conventional or digital will be decided by the added value of the process: for digital printing this includes distributed printing and the ability to vary the image with each copy, while for conventional processes such as litho it will include the higher quality levels, the greater range of substrates that can be printed, and the availability of inline processes such as coating.

Digital Printing Technologies

Digital printers currently fall into four basic types:
- Page printers that print flat sheets of paper, usually in 8.5×11-in. format but sometimes up to 11×17-in.—these range from desktop printers to high-speed copier/printers like DocuTech, and include high-quality continuous-tone printers used mostly for proofs and presentation materials
- Large-format devices that print on continuous rolls, mainly for short-run posters
- Overprinting heads for adding product codes (mainly for packaging) that are mounted onto conventional presses or finishing equipment, or on packaging lines
- Roll-fed machines that print at speeds comparable to conventional printing presses

A digital printer has two fundamental components: a marking engine that transfers colorant to the paper, and a front-end that prepares the data used to drive the marking engine. The front end will include a RIP and a memory buffer. The page data is transferred directly to the front end without the need for films and plates, so there are large potential savings in prepress costs.

Because the digital printing device is driven by data and requires no plates, the image can be changed for each successive print. This "variable image" printing concept has great potential interest to publishers and advertisers who are interested in tailoring their communications more closely to what is known about their audience, often in conjunction with sophisticated marketing databases.

Digital printing systems that operate at high speeds or high resolutions require dedicated front ends and large memory buffers, but low-end devices such as desktop printers can make use of software-based printer drivers that sit on the user's host computer.

The most widely-used technologies in marking engines are inkjet, laser and dye sublimation.

Inkjet. Inkjet printers deploy an array of nozzles to project ink droplets onto the paper surface. The nozzles are relatively cheap to produce, and wider arrays that can image a moving web of paper are currently in development. Inkjet print heads are found in all the types of digital printer listed earlier, and dominate the large-format and overprinting markets. They can print on the widest range of substrates (including cheaper grades).

Laser. Laser printers transfer toner to the paper surface electrostatically. An image is created on a photoconductive surface by adding or removing an electrical charge, and toner is attracted to the charged areas on this imaging surface (laser printers are perhaps more accurately known as electrostatic printers, since other energy sources such as electron beams can also be used to alter the conductive properties of the imaging surface). Most systems use dry toner powder, but liquid toner systems are also available and deliver much better print quality: smaller particle sizes yield higher print resolution, and gloss resins can be incorporated to make the finish more like that of a conventional print. Laser printers are mainly found in page printers and roll-fed printers.

Dye sublimation. Dye sublimation printers vaporize a waxy colorant and transfer it to the paper surface. The unit cost of prints made by this process are extremely high, and as a result its use is restricted largely to one-off prints for proofing or presentation purposes. Quality can be extremely high, comparable to a glossy photographic print.

With all the digital printing systems there is a trade-off between resolution and speed. The more device pixels there are to be imaged on a page, the slower the print speed will be in pages per minute.

Direct-to-press. One of the success stories of digital printing is Heidelberg's Quickmaster DI, which uses digital imaging on an otherwise conventional press design. Machines have been installed in a large number of bureau-type operations, and deliver many of the advantages of digital printing at the quality and cost associated with litho.

**A New
Production
Model**

The traditional model of print production can be summarized as "print a large enough quantity of a product to make unit costs economical, and then distribute to the end-user." Digital technologies make it possible to completely rethink the way in which visual communications are produced and distributed.

Print-on-demand. Because the amount of prepress work and press makeready are minimal when compared with conventional printing, production costs are almost entirely variable, with a very small fixed element. This means that they become cost-effective to print copies as they are needed, instead of producing for stock.

Distribute, then print. Printed products are usually distributed over a wide geographical area, and it can sometimes be more cost-effective to distribute the pages in digital form for local reproduction.

Distribute electronically. For items whose function is information rather than marketing, end-users will often accept the end product in electronic form (on disk or CD): the pages can be printed individually as required. This allows the originator of the product to focus on its content instead of its reproduction.

Alternatively, it may be possible to use an online distribution medium such as the World Wide Web, and create pages that are intended for viewing on screen rather than reproduced on paper.

Variable image printing. As each page is imaged separately, and there is no physical printing plate, it is possible to change some or all of the page with each successive print. This enables, for example, each communication to be personalized for its intended recipient, and groups of readers can then be targeted with information appropriate to their interests, their social background or their geographical location.

11 Quality

Phil Green

The value of a printed piece is closely linked to its quality. The design, the materials used, and the production work (including prepress, printing and finishing) all contribute to the end-user's perception of the finished product and the message it attempts to communicate.

The quality of any printed piece has two dimensions. The first is the degree to which the finished product conforms with the specification and the stated requirements of the customer; this aspect of quality is objective and measurable. The second is its excellence — the degree to which the piece stands out as a way of communicating its message to the intended recipient. While conformance can be achieved by following the right procedures in production and avoiding errors, excellence is attained by innovative design backed up by optimal use of production technology. Aiming for excellence implies a search for continual improvement in the product.

One of the objectives of quality procedures is to avoid substandard products reaching the end-user. Defective copies will always result in material losses to the print purchaser, whether through lost sales, returned products or simply through loss of goodwill. It is essential that a procedure exists to eliminate such copies from the final job, whether through the printer's quality assurance system or through sampling carried out by the print buyer.

Strategies for evaluating print quality, monitoring supplier performance, approving payment, and working with suppliers to achieve continuous improvements in quality are discussed in this chapter.

Control Strips

In a typical printed page containing a mixture of type, graphics and images, it is often difficult to isolate particular print attributes such as the level of inking. To assist the printer to establish the correct inking, and to enable print quality to be checked, a narrow strip of color patches known as a control strip is printed on the back edge of a sheet or section. These patches allow different aspects of print quality to be monitored objectively, and compared with proofs or with agreed production tolerances.

The strips are exposed on the plate during the platemaking process. There are a variety of different designs of strip available from different vendors, including ones designed for use with scanning densitometers (see Figure 11-1). All strips incorporate the same basic patches with minor modifications, and for visual assessment or manual measurement there is little real difference in practice.

A word of warning on using the halftone patches to check attributes such as dot gain — the control strip must be an original film strip and not duplicated. Contacting strips to make duplicates alters the dot sizes and renders any measurements inaccurate. Duplicate strips can be difficult to detect, but a good guide is whether the tiny elements in the tonal value transfer patches have become badly degraded.

Control strips can yield all kinds of information about printing conditions, including the mechanical state of the press itself. Although some data cannot be interpreted without fairly sophisticated analysis and are intended more for internal use by the printer, the strip can be a useful tool for the print buyer, allowing, for example, a means of:

- Checking for shifts in color balance
- Making objective comparisons between running sheets and proofs
- Checking ink weights and other characteristics against agreed standards
- Confirming that prepress adjustments (such as the allowance for dot gain that is made to color separations) are accurate
- Troubleshooting quality problems (see Figure 11-2)

Solid patches are provided to evaluate ink weight. Because ink weight is really the one thing that the press operator controls during a print run, and the one that is most prone to fluctuations, the solid patches appear at frequent intervals along the strip. On strips designed for use with scanning

Figure 11-1.
Transition densitometer for measuring film density. Film control strips for monitoring the exposure level on contact films and plates are also shown. To measure ink density on prints and proofs, reflection densitometers are used.

Figure 11-2.
Detail of control strip instruction for monitoring print quality. *Courtesy of Gretag.*

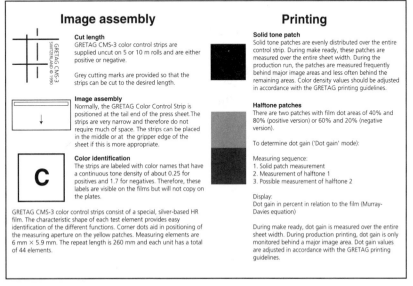

Image assembly

Cut length
GRETAG CMS-3 color control strips are supplied uncut on 5 or 10 m rolls and are either positive or negative.

Grey cutting marks are provided so that the strips can be cut to the desired length.

Image assembly
Normally, the GRETAG Color Control Strip is positioned at the tail end of the press sheet. The strips are very narrow and therefore do not require much of space. The strips can be placed in the middle or at the gripper edge of the sheet if this is more appropriate.

Color identification
The strips are labeled with color names that have a continuous tone density of about 0.25 for positives and 1.7 for negatives. Therefore, these labels are visible on the films but will not copy on the plates.

GRETAG CMS-3 color control strips consist of a special, silver-based HR film. The characteristic shape of each test element provides easy identification of the different functions. Corner dots aid in positioning of the measuring aperture on the yellow patches. Measuring elements are 6 mm × 5.9 mm. The repeat length is 260 mm and each unit has a total of 44 elements.

Printing

Solid tone patch
Solid tone patches are evenly distributed over the entire control strip. During make ready, these patches are measured over the entire sheet width. During the production run, the patches are measured frequently behind major image areas and less often behind the remaining areas. Color density values should be adjusted in accordance with the GRETAG printing guidelines.

Halftone patches
There are two patches with film dot areas of 40% and 80% (positive version) or 60% and 20% (negative version).

To determine dot gain ('Dot gain' mode):

Measuring sequence:
1. Solid patch measurement
2. Measurement of halftone 1
3. Possible measurement of halftone 2

Display:
Dot gain in percent in relation to the film (Murray-Davies equation)

During make ready, dot gain is measured over the entire sheet width. During production printing, dot gain is only monitored behind a major image area. Dot gain values are adjusted in accordance with the GRETAG printing guidelines.

densitometers, their frequency is related to the spacing of the inking controls — roughly every 1.2 in. (30 mm).

Significant variations in ink weight can be seen with the human eye, but for objective measurement a densitometer is needed.

Tone patches provide a basis for measuring dot gain. Spaced less frequently than solid patches, they have a known dot size on film, and by measuring the printed dot size the dot gain can be found.

Tone patches cannot be assessed visually but require a densitometer.

Confusion sometimes occurs in the reading of tone patches because different manufacturers have chosen a different basis for measurement—for example, Gretag strips have 40% and 80% patches, whereas a Brunner strip has 25% and 75% patches. If the densitometer is in dot gain mode (performing the arithmetic internally), care must be taken to ensure that the appropriate reference dot size has been entered. If readings are being taken from a variety of different types of strip, it is simpler to keep the instrument in dot area mode, carrying out the simple subtraction manually to arrive at the dot gain.

The gray balance patch is one of the most useful control elements as it helps in identifying the cause of color casts. The gray balance patch is a mid-tone gray and is made up from roughly equal amounts of the three process colors, cyan, magenta and yellow. Because the eye is much more sensitive to color shifts in neutrals than in saturated colors, the gray balance patch shows up even very small changes in color balance and effectively acts as an early warning of shifts in color.

The balance between the process colors is more critical to achieving a good color match than the overall ink weights, and quite small fluctuations in tonal values caused by a variation in ink weight or dot gain, even if still within their tolerances, can cause noticeable color shifts if they occur in different amounts in cyan, magenta and yellow.

If all three colors are printed in balance, the patch should appear to be a neutral gray similar in appearance to the black tint printed next to it. If one color is printed too light or too heavy it will be obvious from the change in the balance patch; too little yellow, for example, would show up as a shift towards a blue-violet color. Gray balance is usually assessed visually.

The gray balance should more or less match the proof, although the printer may compromise a little to achieve the best color match to the originals or to compensate for slightly different paper or tonal reproduction characteristics from the proof.

Among the other quality attributes that can be assessed from the control strip are slur and tonal value transfer from film to plate.

Slur

Slur is an elongation of the image arising from the mechanical condition of the printing press. It does not occur on a well-adjusted press. It is detected on a control element which has vertical and horizontal lines of the same thickness: the horizontal lines suffer a thickening when slur is present but the vertical ones do not, and as a result the horizontal lines look darker. Different makes of control strip all have different designs of slur targets, but they all serve the same purpose.

Tonal Value

Tonal value transfer refers to the accuracy of plate exposure and the transfer of halftone dots from film to plate. Even when contact between film and plate during exposure is good, a small amount of light finds its way under the film emulsion. On a positive-working plate the image is undercut and sharpened, while on a negative-working plate the opposite happens, the dot becomes larger. The accuracy of this process is monitored by observing the small dots and lines on the tonal value transfer patch on the control strip. Offset plates have a resolving power of around 6 μm, and exposures should be set so that the 2% dot is held and the 10% or 11% lines are unbroken, and smaller elements are breaking up or lost altogether. If this condition is not met, there will be a noticeable shift from the required color values in tints and images.

Control strips should appear on every color job. Occasionally the printer may run a "test form" with a larger range of test patches to characterize the press performance, in order to calibrate prepress equipment or determine the optimum inking for a new type of paper.

Measurement

Some of the most important aspects of print quality can be easily quantified, and making measurements establishes a clear basis for quality standards and acceptance. In the absence of measured data one is forced to rely on subjective judgments that are open to different interpretations and are too easily influenced by external factors such as lighting conditions.

The human visual mechanism of color perception is not designed to make objective color assessments, but rather to recognize objects under a wide range of conditions. As a result it is highly proficient at discriminating between similar colors when seen together, but poor at judging colors independent of the environment. For example, a plain sheet of paper is recognized as white regardless of its surroundings, yet the light it reflects may actually be yellowish (under tungsten), greenish (under fluorescent), bluish (under daylight) or gray (at twilight).

The key variables to monitor in printing were described above: ink weight, dot gain, and color.

Ink Weight

Ink weight is monitored through measurements of the optical density of the ink. There is a good relationship between optical density measurements and both the thickness of the printed ink film and the human perception of lightness. Density is simply the measurement of the proportion of light falling on the paper surface that is absorbed by it, placed on a logarithmic scale to keep the numbers inside sensible bounds and make it closer to the human visual response. White paper normally has a density of around 0.04 (compared with a reference white of zero density used for calibration), while at the other end of the scale the maximum density of most printing processes is around 2.2. These figures correspond to surfaces reflecting 91% and 0.6% of the light they receive respectively.

Dot Gain

Dot gain is measured by simply finding the dot size in a printed halftone (the "apparent dot area") and comparing this with the size of the dot on the films used for platemaking (the "actual dot area"). The dot size is computed from density measurements of the solid, unprinted and halftone areas.

Color

Color is measured using the universally-adopted procedures devised by the CIE (Comité Internationale de l'Éclairage), based on the color vision of a typical human observer. The measurements can be displayed in several different ways (including xyY and XYZ values), but in printing the most widely-used system is CIELAB. Its advantage is that the magnitude of difference between two values corresponds better to the human perception of color differences than most other color spaces, and for this reason is often referred to as a "color difference space." A new variant of this, known as CMC, provides an even more perceptually uniform color difference space and is increasingly being adopted by printers and print buyers.

Other variables are also measured when necessary for troubleshooting. These include factors such as ink purity, ink trap and print contrast.

Just Noticeable Differences

Opinions vary to some degree on what constitutes a barely perceptible difference (a just noticeable difference, or JND) between the variables described above, and factors such as the ink color will have an influence. However, most people agree that 0.1 density units is the smallest density difference that is perceptible; similarly, 1% dot gain is considered just noticeable, as is a 2 ΔE difference in CIELAB values.

These JNDs are important as they help us set a tolerance for acceptance. Since a solid color whose density differs from the proof by more than 0.1 will be visibly different, this value acts as a useful limit of what is acceptable. Similarly, it is usual to make 2% dot gain the tolerance limit. With color measurements it is accepted that it is much harder to maintain a production tolerance of 2 ΔE units, so a larger tolerance of up to 6–8 ΔE units is often agreed.

Virtually all industry standards incorporate the 0.1 density and 2% gain tolerances. Currently there is no standard for color tolerance, and this is a matter for negotiation between printer and buyer. Tolerances should not be set tighter than necessary unless the additional expense of achieving them can be justified.

The forthcoming ISO standard on process control for printing (ISO 12647, currently in draft form) specifies color tolerances, including solid ink weights, in terms of CIELAB values. In everyday use, however, density measurements remain the most useful way of measuring, communicating, and controlling ink weights.

The Instruments

Densitometer. The densitometer is the most widely used instrument, largely owing to its relatively low cost and its suitability for monitoring press inking. The instrument consists essentially of a light source, an aperture and a photo cell; by sending light to the substrate and measuring the amount that is reflected back to the photocell, the reflectance and thus the density can be recorded. Microprocessors inside the instrument are programmed to carry out the dot gain calculation and a range of other functions.

A densitometer does not measure the color of a surface but simply its reflectance. A densitometer that is used in process color printing is equipped with four filters that the reflected light passes through before reaching the photocell. One filter (for measuring black) is neutral in color; the remaining three have colors that are more or less complementary to the three process colors cyan, magenta and yellow.

Transmission densitometers shine light from beneath the substrate instead of above it, allowing them to measure the density of transparent and translucent materials. They are essential when measuring the densities of film emulsions.

For most purposes in the assessment of printed products, a relatively simple reflection densitometer with just density and dot gain readings is sufficient. Additional functions carry a high price premium, and in practice tend to be used very infrequently. Setting up the other functions on a spreadsheet is very straightforward, and may well be preferable to spending in excess of $1650 (£1000) to get the additional functionality in the instrument.

Density measurements taken with different instruments rarely agree exactly, usually for one of three reasons:
- The filters or the internal light source may have aged, causing the readings to drift
- They may incorporate different types of filters
- Users do not always recalibrate their instruments as recommended
- Manufacturers use different techniques to set up their instruments, so that while, for example, all Gretag densitometers may give similar readings, they may be different from the readings from Macbeth devices

The widest variations come from the use of different filter types. Most manufacturers and standards bodies have settled on ANSI Status T for densitometer filters. The filter sets in use generally incorporate polarization, which removes the "glossy component" that makes wet ink give higher density readings than dry ink, with the result that a filter with polarization will give you the same reading on both wet and dry sheets. This avoids the misleading effects of observing wet ink before it dries and inevitably appears duller.

Spectrophotometer. Like the densitometer, the spectrophotometer measures the amount of light reflected back to its collector photocell, but measures the reflectance right across the visible spectrum so that the color can be defined precisely. Older instruments used filters to separate the spectrum into different bands of wavelengths, but now most devices use a diffraction grating for greater reliability and lower production cost.

Increasing interest in color measurement among graphic designers, printers and publishers, in addition to existing users in the fields of packaging and papermaking, has led to new models appearing that are aimed at these new markets. The increasing volume is enabling manufacturers to reduce prices to much more competitive levels, making color measurement a genuinely affordable option for print buyers with a need to evaluate color quality.It should be noted that some of the cheapest devices have poor reliability.

Spectrophotometers can present their measurements as CIE xyY, XYZ, L*a*b*, or L'u'v' readings (to mention just a few), and can also show a spectral reflectance curve (a graph showing the amount of light reflected at each wavelength) for the color being measured. They are often equipped with additional software that assists in color matching decisions, and in some cases with the ability to display density and dot gain readings, allowing them to be used in place of a densitometer.

Spectrophotometry is a complex field, and users should have some knowledge of color theory to use the instruments and interpret their results in a meaningful way.

When density or color measurements are being made as part of real-time process control (instead of their more common use in comparing proofs with makeready sheets and occasional inspection sheets during the run), sheets are being continually assessed as they are printed and the action of manually taking a reading and recording it is too slow. For this purpose, scanning densitometers and spectrophotometers continually traverse the sheet taking readings, which are displayed on a screen. They can be linked to the press control system, enabling the press to respond to color variations by making adjustments in inking levels. They can also analyze the readings and print reports on the performance of the press.

Other essential tools for quality control include linen testers, color viewing cabinets, and printed tint charts for checking dot sizes.

Acceptance

You will normally have seen a final proof of a job before it is printed, but if it has a high value, or if there are critical elements that you want to monitor closely, it is a good practice to ask for a set of running sheets as soon as printing has finished. Binding will probably not commence until several hours after the last section has been printed to give the ink time to dry, and this is a good opportunity for a final check before the sections are bound together. If a disastrous error is spotted before binding has taken place, it will be possible to reprint that sheet alone, whereas if the error is not picked up until you receive finished copies, it can only be corrected by reprinting the entire job.

As well as seeing a finished copy of the job, you will want assurance that the whole run has been produced to the same standard. It is not completely unknown for printers to pull out the best examples as file copies for delivery to the buyer, leaving a question mark over the remainder of the run. You can determine if this has happened quite easily by comparing the ink weight in a color solid on each copy with a densitometer — if they are identical they were almost certainly printed consecutively.

If you have confidence in the printer's quality assurance systems, you may be content to place your trust in their ability to deliver a completely consistent product to you; otherwise you may want to have some evidence that the level of consistency is acceptable. The press operator will have pulled out copies during the run, at intervals of around 500 to 1000 impressions, and a full set of these may be available for inspection, especially if you make this requirement part of your regular working practice. In addition to inspecting each sheet for cleanliness and freedom from defects, you can visually evaluate inking by fanning the sheets out with an overlap of about 0.6 in. (15 mm) so that color areas are shingled for easy comparison.

After the job has been accepted, it is a good practice to note down anything that bears on the product quality, timeliness of delivery, and any extra costs. The reasons for doing this are:
- To enable you to maintain records on the performance of your suppliers
- To make sure you have all the relevant information when you negotiate with the printer
- So that you can report to whoever will authorize payment in your organization, explaining any additional items

Printing Faults   What kinds of defect can occur in printing, and how do you decide who is responsible?

To list all the faults that can appear on a printed piece would require a separate book, as there are so many variables involved. Good design is innovative and as a result virtually every print job is unique; the highly complex physical and chemical interactions between press, paper, ink and varnish means that sometimes faults arise that even the most experienced printer could not have been expected to predict.

Any deviation between the proof and the final pressrun can be considered as a defect. The most common reasons for variations are:

• Proof characteristics not matching the press characteristics
• Different ink weights
• Different substrate
• Changes being made inadvertently after proofing
• Inadequate quality control over platemaking

This first group of faults will normally affect the whole print run. Faults you are most likely to encounter during the pressrun are:

• Color variations
• Spots
• Marking
• Misregister

Marking can be of two kinds: vertical (i.e., in the direction of travel), usually caused by wet ink touching a part of the press as it moves through the machine, and horizontal, generally caused by mechanical defects in the press. Another kind of mark appears when wet ink is allowed to "setoff" onto facing sheets.

A small degree of misregister is inevitable as paper expands during printing, and should be allowed for in the design. Register tolerances will depend on the paper type and sheet size.

Spots are mostly caused by dirt from one source or another.

This second group of faults may only appear on a small number of copies before the operator corrects them, or they may come and go through the run. You may need to sample the run carefully to get a picture of how many copies are affected.

No pressrun ever matches the proof perfectly, and you will need to find out what the printer's normal tolerances are, or agree to them with the printer. In the majority of commercial color work it is not economical to set tolerances too closely, while in certain kinds of printing (such as pharmaceuticals and packaging generally) accurate color reproduction may have a much greater legal or economic significance.

Finally, a wide range of possible faults can arise in the finishing stage, during the process of coating, folding, securing or cutting the finished copies. These may be caused by a failure in the finishing operation itself, or by some combination of factors (such as attempting to cut sheets that have not dried, or laminating onto an ink or paper surface that is unsuitable).

Unless the inputs you have supplied are defective in some way (if, for example, you have specified an unsuitable paper, or if the proof you have supplied is not a realistic simulation of what can be achieved on press), faults like the ones described above are the printer's responsibility. Where there is a clear risk of a serious fault occurring, as might be the case if you asked for a fast turnaround that did not allow time for the ink to dry, for example, you should normally expect the printer to anticipate the problem and warn you.

Quality Control or Quality Assurance?

Quality control is largely based on the inspection of finished goods to ensure that the quality is satisfactory. Inspecting printed copies is not the best use of a print buyer's time, and if defects are discovered it may already be too late to fix them. A quality assurance approach puts the emphasis on prevention rather than cure, and on setting up well-defined procedures that should ensure conformance with the designs and specifications supplied. From the buyer's point of view, the main objective of quality assurance is to place the responsibility for quality where it belongs, which is with the supplier. This means that the printer has to ensure that every single copy printed meets the requirements of the client, documenting the procedures required to achieve this and carrying out any checking that may be needed. Note, however, that it also means that the buyer has to ensure that anything supplied to the printer (in the form of artwork, photographic originals, specifications and instructions or material such as paper) must also be of an adequate standard.

The underlying assumption of quality assurance is that if all the inputs are right, and the process is functioning correctly, then the finished product should conform to the design and specification.

Increasing numbers of printers have adopted the internationally-recognized quality assurance standard ISO 9000 (the standard has been adopted by most industrial countries). This lays down a detailed set of procedures that must be thoroughly documented and externally validated to achieve certification under the standard.

On the whole, ISO 9000-certified companies tend to be more rigorous in their approach to quality, although the purpose of quality assurance is sometimes misunderstood; it is intended to be a guarantee of conformance with design and specification rather than a sign of quality in the sense in which it is commonly used (meaning excellence). A company could produce work that was consistently mediocre and still of the standard quality. In printing, excellence is ultimately achieved by skilled individuals who are motivated, well managed, and equipped with the right tools and equipment, rather than by the effect of policies and procedures alone.

One of the greatest contributions the buyer can make to print quality is to insist on design that is robust rather than fragile. Robust designs are those that can tolerate minor variations during the production process without causing objectionable defects. Fragile designs, on the other hand, are those where visible defects result from small variations in the process. For example, printing 6-point type reversed white out of three colors on a large sheet size requires the colors to be registered perfectly, and the inevitable expansion of the paper between colors during printing is virtually guaranteed to make the type unreadable. Overprinting the type, or dropping it out of just one color, would in this case make the design much more robust as a small variation in register would have no effect on it.

Given the time and the resources, a printer can reproduce more or less anything the designer can create. The difference is that robust design is less prone to errors and inevitably costs less to print.

You should also carefully examine all the material that is to be sent to the printer, to ensure that the relevant guidelines have been followed. The printer will be able to advise you, and tell you whether any house requirements or published standards apply. They may cover:
• The suitability of paper and board

- The compatibility of inks and special finishes such as varnishes and laminations
- The preparation of electronic artwork
- The quality of photographic originals (transparencies and prints)
- The procedure to follow when marking up proofs

If you can assure the printer that everything you submit is of a suitable quality, you can be more confident of the quality of the final job.

The quality assurance philosophy can be applied to other areas of the print production process, including creation and management functions. The maximum benefits are realized when it is applied right through the production chain.

Statistical Process Control

The manufacturing industry has increasingly adopted statistical methods of analyzing production performance as the technology has become available to collect the data automatically from the process, and to apply sophisticated computation to the results. Statistical process control (SPC) is often a key element in total quality management (TQM) programs, and its value has been proven in many different fields.

SPC enables both the printer and the print buyer to determine whether a process is capable of meeting quality requirements, to analyze its performance in detail, and also provides the operator with the means to adjust the process correctly.

Some of the SPC tools that are applied to printing are:

- Control charts (which record the print variables being monitored over time and compare them to agreed tolerance values)
- Pareto analysis (which ranks defects according to their frequency and highlights the areas needing attention)
- Histogram analysis (which shows the way that variations are distributed)

Print buyers can use the results of SPC analyses to review or audit the performance of their suppliers.

Some presses are equipped with more sophisticated monitoring equipment that records the readings from the built-in densitometer or spectrophotometer, and produces reports for the printer's management information system at the end of the run. These reports include statistical analysis of the run, and are used by the printer to monitor quality control. If these reports are capable of being generated by the printer's system, it is quite reasonable for the buyer to request a copy for a job that is in progress. The printer may also be willing to supply the results of other analyses, or even to work with the print purchaser on quality reviews with the objective of bringing about consistent, long-term improvements in quality.

Working with the Printer

There is no reason for a printer to want to produce substandard work, and every reason for them to do the best they possibly can. The printer is strongly motivated by client goodwill, the need to avoid costly disputes, and even by personal pride; the printer invariably wants to turn out the best work they possibly can for their clients.

An experienced print buyer can use this as a starting point in developing a relationship with a printer. Through a long-term relationship with a supplier you can establish the standards of quality that you require, and the type of service that you expect.

It is good practice to hold regular meetings with your suppliers, where you can discuss problems that have occurred in recent work and also how you can work together to continue to improve the quality of what you do.

By using the printer's expertise it is possible to add value to a printed piece without incurring extra costs, for example the printer may be able to suggest ways in which an advantage could be taken from a particular page imposition, or how additional colors can be used for little or no cost. Paper and ink makers are also a useful source of information on the suitability of their products for different uses.

Among the objectives of the buyer in working with a printer on any printed piece are to:

- Satisfy the requirements of the product at the lowest possible cost
- Create a smooth and harmonious workflow that aids the printer to meet delivery dates and ensures that errors are intercepted at the earliest possible stage
- Achieve continuous improvements in the standard of work

Printers regularly evaluate and adopt innovations in production technology and working methods, and the print buyer should keep up to date with the latest developments. A printer's decision on whether to invest in a particular technology is often based on demand from their customers, especially if there is no immediate commercial benefit to the printer.

Responding to Defects

It is good policy to bring all but the most trivial defects to the attention of the printer as soon as they are noticed. Ignoring errors sends out the wrong message, implying that you are prepared to accept substandard work. Raising all problems with the printer creates an opportunity to establish and re-iterate the standard you require; it is also useful for the printer to know where the limits are drawn so that errors can be dealt with internally without emerging into the cold light of day.

Resolving a quality problem can be one of the more difficult negotiations that a print buyer has to undertake. You will need to be firm about what you know to be the problem, but open to suggestions that the printer might make about how to overcome it.

You might want to prepare yourself for this negotiation by:

- Determining what procedures should have been followed (referring to a copy of the printer's quality policy and procedure manuals if available)
- Ensuring that you have a reasonable technical understanding of the nature and cause of the defect, or a colleague who does who can be present to advise you during the negotiations
- Establishing what standards and tolerances should have been in force, and having available copies of any measurements that were made on the job in question

Monetary compensation may not always be the aim of the negotiation — you may simply want the printer to acknowledge the problem and prevent its reoccurrence. If there is agreement that the job is unacceptable the printer will normally prefer to reprint the offending work; alternatively, if this is not realistic (owing to factors such as the pressure of distribution time scales) or necessary, you may be offered a discount on future work or some other value-added service in lieu of a reduction on the cost of the present job, and in some cases this may be satisfactory. Where monetary compensation is your objective, however, a reasonable guideline is a reduction corresponding to the print and paper costs of the defective pages on a pro rata basis. If advertising is involved, any lost ad revenue should also be claimed.

You may also be entitled to claim any other financial losses that you have incurred as a result of the error (such as the value of sales lost by the reduced print quality), although in practice it can be difficult to prove such consequential losses.

In most cases you will be in a position to simply withhold payment of all or part of the invoice for a job that has been printed badly. This is a weapon that should be used only when absolutely necessary, as it will damage any relationship that you have built up, and possibly lead to the restriction of credit facilities for future work. It is essential to make every effort to reach an agreement with the printer before taking unilateral action.

If a dispute cannot be resolved you may have to take further action. If the printer is being particularly recalcitrant, you may have no other solution but to take them to court, although the costs of doing so are likely to outweigh any compensation you may receive. It is much better to use an arbitration service (such as those provided by the Better Business Bureau and Pira International), as this will give a fair resolution at a far lower cost.

Achieving excellence and value in print has been a focus throughout this book. Some of the key points to emphasize here in conclusion to this chapter are:

- Plan to get the result you want, with the maximum value for money that the process can provide.
- Use suppliers that you are confident can produce the quality you want.
- Develop good working relationships and information flows with your suppliers.
- Define the quality criteria for each job, and monitor these criteria from the design through to the finished job.
- Make certain that the design meets the client's requirements, and can be produced efficiently, before the job goes into production.
- Specify the finished product accurately.
- Choose the right originals, and mark them up so that the printer can see how you want them to print.
- Choose the most appropriate materials for the job.
- Choose the most appropriate proofing system, and check the proofs carefully.
- Make the most of the printer's desire to help you to produce a quality product that has the maximum value to you.

Bibliography

Appleton, B. *Screen Printing*. Pira International: 1994.

Bann, B. *The Print Production Handbook*. Macdonald: 1986.

Bann, D. and Gargan, J. *Colour Proof Correction*. Phaidon: 1990.

Barnard, M. *Introduction to Print Buying*. Blueprint Publishing: 1989.

———. *Magazine and Journal Production*. Blueprint Publishing: 1986.

———. *Introduction to Printing Processes*. Blueprint Publishing: 1991.

Birkenshaw, J. *Finishing for the Customer*. Pira International: 1995.

Dale, B.G. and Plunkett, J.J. (eds.) *Managing Quality*. Philip Alan: 1990.

Eves, I. *Publisher's Guide to Paper*. Blueprint Publishing: 1988.

Field, G. *Color and its Reproduction*. Graphic Arts Technical Foundation: 1988.

Fink, P. *PostScript Screening*. Adobe Press: 1992.

Flexography—Principles and Practice. Flexographic Technical Association: 1988.

Green, P.J. *Understanding Digital Color*. Graphic Arts Technical Foundation: 1995.

———. *Quality Control for Print Buyers*. Blueprint Publishing: 1992.

Holmes, K. *Pira Guide to Total Quality Management*. Pira International: 1992.

International Printing Sourcebook. Pira International. 1995.

Introduction to Printing Technology. British Printing Industries Federation: 1993.

Jamieson, A. *The Print and Packaging Buying Handbook*. Blueprint Publishing: 1996.

Johnson, T. and Scott-Taggart, M. *Guidelines for Choosing the Correct Viewing Conditions for Colour Publishing*. Pira International: 1994.

Jönson, G. *LCA – A Tool for Measuring Environmental Performance*. Pira International: 1996.

Leach, R.H. *The Printing Ink Manual* (5th edition). Van Nostrand Reinhold International/Blueprint Publishing: 1988.

Magee, B. *Screen Printing Primer*. Graphic Arts Technical Foundation: 1985.

Martin, G. *Nonimpact Printing*. Pira International: 1993.

Mortimer, A. *Colour Page Make-up Systems*. Pira International: 1995.

———. *Colour Reproduction in the Printing Industry*. Pira International: 1990.

Mulvihill, D. *Flexography Primer*. Graphic Arts Technical Foundation: 1985.

Nemoto, M. *Total Quality Control for Management*. Prentice Hall: 1987.

Nothmann, G. *Nonimpact Printing*. Graphic Arts Technical Foundation: 1989.

Oakland, J. *Statistical Process Control*. Heinemann (1986)

———. *Total Quality Management*. Butterworth Heinemann: 1989.

Paper Specifications and the Paper Buyer. British Printing Industries Federation: 1990.

Paper Testing Standards. Technical Association of the Pulp and Paper Industry.

Peacock, J. *Book Production.* Blueprint Publishing and the Publishers Association: 1989.

Potter, G. *Binding and Finishing.* Blueprint Publishing: 1988.

Price, F. *Right First Time.* Gower: 1985.

Saltman, D. *Lithography Primer.* Graphic Arts Technical Foundation: 1986.

Smith, H.B. *Modern Gravure Technology.* Pira International: 1994.

Standardising Process Colour Printing. British Printing Industries Federation: 1982.

Stephens, J. *Screen Process Printing—A Practical Guide.* Blueprint Publishing: 1987.

Stevenson, D. *Handbook of Printing Processes.* Graphic Arts Technical Foundation: 1994.

Tritton, K. *Pira Guide to Colour Control in Lithography.* Pira International: 1993.

White, T. *High Quality Flexography.* Pira International: 1992.

Appendix: Organizations

Standards Bodies

American National Standards Institute (ANSI)
11 West 42nd Street
New York, NY 10036
Ph: 212/642-4900
Fax: 212/398-0023

British Standards Institution (BSI)
389 Chiswick High Road
London W4 4AL
UK
Ph: (+44) (0) 181 996 9000
Fax: (+44) (0) 181 996 7400

Commission International de l'Eclairage (CIE)
57 Rue Curier
Paris 5, France

International Standards Organization
1 Rue de Varembe
1 211 Geneva 20
Switzerland
Ph: (+41) 22 341240
Fax: (+41) 22 333430

(ISO standards are also available from national standards bodies.)

Research and Technical Organizations

Graphic Arts Technical Foundation
200 Deer Run Road
Sewickley, PA 15143
Ph: 412/741-6860
Fax: 412/741-2311

Pira International
Randalls Road
Leatherhead
Surrey KT22 7RU
UK
Ph: (+44) 01372 802050
Fax: (+44) 01372 802239

Purchaser's Organizations

American Association of Advertising Agencies
666 Third Avenue
New York, NY 10017
Ph: 212/682-2500
Fax: 212/682-2500

Association of Print and Packaging Buyers
10 Ridgeway Road
Redhill
Surrey RH1 6PH
UK
Ph: 01737 780 150
Fax: 01737 880 160

Institute of Practitioners in Advertising
44 Belgrave Square
London SW1X 8QS
UK

International Federation of the Periodical Press (FIPP)
Press Foundation House
5 Matthew Street
London SW1P 2JT
UK

Magazine Publishers of America
575 Lexington Avenue
New York, NY 10022
Ph: 212/752-0055
Fax: 212/888-4217

Periodical Publishers Association
Imperial House
15–19 Kingsway
London WC2B 6UN
UK
Ph: (+44) 171 836 8798
Fax: (+44) 171 379 5661

Supplier Organizations

British Paper and Board Industry Federation
Papermakers House
Riverhill Road
Westlea
Swindon
Wiltshire SN5 7BE
UK
Ph: (+44) 1793 886086
Fax: (+44) 1793 886182

British Printing Industry Federation
11 Bedford Row
London WC1R 4DX
UK
Ph: (+44) 171 242 6904
Fax: (+44) 171 405 7784

European Flexographic Technical Association
6 The Tynings
Clevedon
Bristol BS21 7YP
UK
Ph: (+44) 1179 246965
Fax: (+44) 1179 246965

Flexographic Technical Association
900 Marconi Avenue
Ronkonkoma, NY 11779
Ph: 516/737-6020
Fax: 516/737-6813

Gravure Association of America
1200-A Scottsville Road
Rochester, NY 14624
Ph: 716/436-2150
Fax: 716/436-7689

International Prepress Association
552 West 167th Street
South Holland, IL 60473
Ph: 612/896-1908
Fax: 612/896-0181

Printing Industries of America
100 Daingerfeld Road
Arlington, VA 22314
Ph: 703/519-8100
Fax: 703/548-3227

Screen Printing Association International
10015 Main Street
Fairfax, VA 22031
Ph: 703/385-1335
Fax: 703/273-0456

Technical Association of the Pulp and Paper Industry
P.O. Box 105113
Atlanta, GA 30348
Ph: 404/446-1400
Fax: 404/446-6947

Biographies

Chris Conolly-Smith

Senior lecturer, Kingston Business School

Chris Conolly-Smith operated at director level in the publishing industry within Reed International plc for many years, responsible for purchasing, strategy and acquisitions. He was later a founding director of Boxtree Ltd, and a director of Pinter Publishers Ltd.

He has operated overseas in many countries on publishing development projects, for the World Bank and Know-How Fund projects. These countries include Russia, Hungary, Poland, Romania, Bulgaria, Albania, Indonesia, Angola, Sierra Leone and South Africa. He is Senior Lecturer in Finance and Small Business at Kingston Business School, and advises publishing and media industry clients on business planning, strategic marketing and corporate financial issues. He regularly chairs the Pira International seminar "Professional Print Buying."

Fax: (+44) (0) 1932 867170
E-mail: c.conolly-smith@kingston.ac.uk

Phil Green

Senior lecturer, London College of Printing and Distributive Trades

Phil Green has a master's degree from the University of Surrey. He spent 13 years in the printing industry, in a variety of production and management positions ranging from film planner to press operator and production manager, before joining the London College of Printing as a lecturer in 1986. Recently he has focused on issues around digital color reproduction, and published *Understanding Digital Color* in 1995. He has run a series of seminars for print buyers since 1985, and has also written *Recycled Paper: a Guide for Printers* and *Quality Control for Print Buyers*. He is currently working on research into device-independent color reproduction.

Tel: (+44) (0) 171 514 6500
E-mail: 100277.3163@compuserve.com

Tony Johnson

Consultant

Tony Johnson entered the printing industry as an apprentice hot metal compositor. Realizing, after a while, that the future may be somewhat limited he finished his apprenticeship and then studied printing technology at the London College of Printing. From there he went to Imperial College to undertake postgraduate studies in color physics and then studied mathematics with the Open University.

He returned to industry in 1970 as assistant production manager at a book printing company in Kent. In 1973 he joined Pira where he undertook research in color reproduction combined with consultancy and training activities. He also became research manager in the printing division. In 1983 he joined Crosfield Electronics Ltd. as research manager and continued his personal interest in color reproduction. In 1994 he was awarded the Gold Medal of the Institute of Printing and in 1995 the TAGA Honors award. Both awards are made for technical contributions to the graphic arts industries.

In 1995 he left Crosfield to set up his own consultancy service to provide advice and training in many technical areas, and at all levels, in graphic arts.

Tel / Fax: (+44) (0) 1296 660100
E-mail: tony@colouruk.demon.co.uk.

Deborah Kamofsky

Commercial director, Anderson Fraser Ltd.

Deborah Kamofsky took an honors degree in graphic communication at the London College of Printing, and worked in the public relations, training and travel industries before completing further studies in management science, business and marketing.

Having worked as a designer, a travel industry print buyer, an independent print broker, and then in both production and account management within a medium-sized print company, she has experienced the print buying process from many points of view.

She is currently the commercial director of Anderson Fraser (litho printers), which she joined in 1988.

Tel: (+44) (0) 171 278 9703

John Stephens

Dean, School of Printing Technology, London College of Printing and Distributive Trades

John Stephens is a leading subject specialist in screen process printing. He joined the industry in 1960 and has wide experience in commercial and creative applications of the process. He was the cofounder of Serigraphic Arts (fine art printers) and Master Printer at the Royal College of Art. He is the author of *Screen Process Printing,* published by Blueprint.

Tel: (+44) (0) 171 514 6500

Wilfried E. Wagner

Consultant, Wagner Partners, UK

Wilfried Wagnerhas a degree in print technology and plant management from the Graphic Arts Academy in Munich. He has lived in England for over 20 years, working as an independent consultant since 1992.

He is a specialist in print and packaging procurement, his earlier career being in print production with Avon Europe where he was later to become director of operations support, with responsibility for developing and coordinating all European and global purchasing.

His consultancy specializes in:
- Determining the effectiveness of buying operations
- Implementing the best purchasing practices
- Developing appropriate buying strategies

His clients come from international direct selling organizations, government departments, insurances and charities.

Wagner is a regular lecturer in professional print buying at Pira International.

Tel: (+44) (0) 1604 870 229
Fax: (+44) (0) 1604 870 470

Index

About GATF

The Graphic Arts Technical Foundation is a nonprofit, scientific, technical, and educational organization dedicated to the advancement of the graphic communications industries worldwide. Its mission is to serve the field as the leading resource for technical information and services through research and education.

For 73 years the Foundation has developed leading edge technologies and practices for printing. GATF's staff of researchers, educators, and technical specialists partner with nearly 2,000 corporate members in over 65 countries to help them maintain their competitive edge by increasing productivity, print quality, process control, and environmental compliance, and by implementing new techniques and technologies. Through conferences, satellite symposia, workshops, consulting, technical support, laboratory services, and publications, GATF strives to advance a global graphic communications community.

The Foundation publishes books on nearly every aspect of the field; learning modules (step-by-step instruction booklets); audiovisuals (CD-ROMs, videocassettes, slides, and audiocassettes); and research and technology reports. It also publishes *GATFWorld,* a bimonthly magazine of technical articles, industry news, and reviews of specific products.

For more information on GATF products and services, please visit our website http://www.gatf.lm.com or write to us at 200 Deer Run Road, Sewickley, PA 15143-2328 (phone: 412/741-6860).

Other Books
of Interest
Available from
GATF

The Graphic Arts Technical Foundation (GATF) is a major publisher of books on printing and related topics. Following are some of GATF's more popular titles:

- *Understanding Digital Color* by Phil Green

- *Guide to Desktop Publishing* by James Cavuoto and Steven Beale

- *On-Demand Printing: The Revolution in Digital and Customized Printing* by Howard Fenton, Frank Kanonik, and Frank Romano

- *Understanding Electronic Communications: Printing in the Electronic Age* by A'isha Ajayi and Pamela Groff

- *GATF Glossary of Graphic Arts Terms* compiled by Pamela Groff

- *Handbook of Printing Processes* by Deborah Stevenson

- *Screen Printing Primer* by Babette Magee

- *Flexography Primer* by Donna Mulvihill

- *Lithography Primer* by David Saltman and Nina Forsythe

- *The Magazine: Everything You Need to Know to Make It in the Magazine Business* by Leonard Mogul